SYNTHETIC DRUGS, REAL DANGER

HEARING

BEFORE THE

SUBCOMMITTEE ON CRIME, TERRORISM, HOMELAND SECURITY, AND INVESTIGATIONS

OF THE

COMMITTEE ON THE JUDICIARY
HOUSE OF REPRESENTATIVES

ONE HUNDRED FOURTEENTH CONGRESS

SECOND SESSION

MAY 17, 2016

Serial No. 114–66

Printed for the use of the Committee on the Judiciary

Available via the World Wide Web: http://judiciary.house.gov

U.S. GOVERNMENT PUBLISHING OFFICE

20–165 PDF   WASHINGTON : 2016

For sale by the Superintendent of Documents, U.S. Government Publishing Office
Internet: bookstore.gpo.gov   Phone: toll free (866) 512–1800; DC area (202) 512–1800
Fax: (202) 512–2104   Mail: Stop IDCC, Washington, DC 20402–0001

COMMITTEE ON THE JUDICIARY

BOB GOODLATTE, Virginia, *Chairman*

F. JAMES SENSENBRENNER, JR.,
 Wisconsin
LAMAR S. SMITH, Texas
STEVE CHABOT, Ohio
DARRELL E. ISSA, California
J. RANDY FORBES, Virginia
STEVE KING, Iowa
TRENT FRANKS, Arizona
LOUIE GOHMERT, Texas
JIM JORDAN, Ohio
TED POE, Texas
JASON CHAFFETZ, Utah
TOM MARINO, Pennsylvania
TREY GOWDY, South Carolina
RAUL LABRADOR, Idaho
BLAKE FARENTHOLD, Texas
DOUG COLLINS, Georgia
RON DeSANTIS, Florida
MIMI WALTERS, California
KEN BUCK, Colorado
JOHN RATCLIFFE, Texas
DAVE TROTT, Michigan
MIKE BISHOP, Michigan

JOHN CONYERS, JR., Michigan
JERROLD NADLER, New York
ZOE LOFGREN, California
SHEILA JACKSON LEE, Texas
STEVE COHEN, Tennessee
HENRY C. "HANK" JOHNSON, JR.,
 Georgia
PEDRO R. PIERLUISI, Puerto Rico
JUDY CHU, California
TED DEUTCH, Florida
LUIS V. GUTIERREZ, Illinois
KAREN BASS, California
CEDRIC RICHMOND, Louisiana
SUZAN DelBENE, Washington
HAKEEM JEFFRIES, New York
DAVID N. CICILLINE, Rhode Island
SCOTT PETERS, California

SHELLEY HUSBAND, *Chief of Staff & General Counsel*
PERRY APELBAUM, *Minority Staff Director & Chief Counsel*

SUBCOMMITTEE ON CRIME, TERRORISM, HOMELAND SECURITY, AND INVESTIGATIONS

F. JAMES SENSENBRENNER, JR., Wisconsin, *Chairman*
LOUIE GOHMERT, Texas, *Vice-Chairman*

STEVE CHABOT, Ohio
J. RANDY FORBES, Virginia
TED POE, Texas
JASON CHAFFETZ, Utah
TREY GOWDY, South Carolina
RAUL LABRADOR, Idaho
KEN BUCK, Colorado
MIKE BISHOP, Michigan

SHEILA JACKSON LEE, Texas
PEDRO R. PIERLUISI, Puerto Rico
JUDY CHU, California
LUIS V. GUTIERREZ, Illinois
KAREN BASS, California
CEDRIC RICHMOND, Louisiana

CAROLINE LYNCH, *Chief Counsel*
JOE GRAUPENSPERGER, *Minority Counsel*

(II)

CONTENTS

MAY 17, 2016

Page

SYNTHETIC DRUGS, REAL DANGER

TUESDAY, MAY 17, 2016

House of Representatives

Subcommittee on Crime, Terrorism,
Homeland Security, and Investigations

Committee on the Judiciary

Washington, DC.

The Subcommittee met, pursuant to call, at 10 a.m., in room 2141, Rayburn House Office Building, the Honorable Ken Buck, (acting Chairman of the Subcommittee) presiding.

Present: Representatives Buck, Goodlatte, Gohmert, Bishop, Labrador, Conyers, Jackson Lee, and Chu.

Staff Present: (Majority) Robert Parmiter, Counsel; Scott Johnson, Clerk; Zachary Somers, Parliamentarian & General Counsel; (Minority) Joe Graupensperger, Minority Counsel; and Veronica Eligan, Professional Staff Member.

Mr. Buck. The Crime, Terrorism, Homeland Security, and Investigations Subcommittee will come to order. Without objection, the Chair is authorized to declare recesses of the Subcommittee at any time. We welcome everyone to this morning's hearing on synthetic drugs, and I will begin by recognizing myself for an opening statement.

Last week, the House took significant steps forward in combating the opioid epidemic in America. Today, this Subcommittee will examine a related but equally important issue: the scourge of synthetic drugs in the United States. Simply put, synthetic drugs are a prime example of how criminals can stay one step ahead of law enforcement.

Today, parents have to worry not only about a child's exposure to illegal drugs, but about synthetic drugs, many of which are produced and marketed directly at children and young adults. Synthetic cannabinoids, with names like Spice, K2, or Scooby Snax, come in brightly-colored packaging, often containing cartoon characters or other decorations to make them attractive to teenagers.

Additionally, they are being marketed and sold as legal alternatives to marijuana, cocaine, and heroin. Thus young people believe them to be safe, legal alternatives. However, they are addictive and deadly. That is because these drugs while designed to mimic the effects of certain illegal drugs, often contain a panoply of additional chemicals which can cause increased heart rate, psychosis, and death.

The professor who is widely credited with first synthesizing cannabinoids for research purposes, Dr. John Huffman of Clemson University, has said, "These things are dangerous. Anybody who uses them is playing Russian roulette. They have profound psychological effects. We never intended them for human consumption." Indeed, they are often labeled as not for human consumption. But everyone, the manufacturer, seller, and the user, knows they are intended to be consumed. Many States have banned these substances by adding them to their controlled substance schedules which has resulted in a patchwork of State laws. Congress has also legislatively scheduled some of these substances, most recently in 2012.

However, the problem is that as soon as the substance is scheduled, or the process begins to schedule a substance, the manufacturers of these illicit drugs simply change a single atom, and the substance is different, and no longer a scheduled substance. Its chemical makeup has been altered slightly, and though it may have the same effect on the body, it is no longer the same chemically. The process has been short circuited. However, the need for a Federal response remains clear, since most synthetic drugs are manufactured and imported overseas, especially from China.

In just a month, in 2014, synthetic marijuana poisoned more than 200 people in my home State of Colorado and killed at least one. The Arapahoe County District Attorney George Brauchler described people trying to cut their own heads off and set themselves on fire after using synthetic drugs. In my State, these drugs have been marketed as synthetic marijuana, and sold at tobacco shops and convenience stores often for a profit of 300 percent or more. It is big business and these manufacturers are profiting off of our misery.

I thank the witnesses for appearing before the Subcommittee today and look forward to their participation. I now recognize the Ranking Member of the full Committee, Mr. Conyers from Michigan, for his opening statement.

Mr. CONYERS. Thank you, Mr. Chairman, and I welcome the witnesses. I look forward to an important discussion. We are going to talk about synthetic drugs, a problem that is primarily affecting adolescents and young adults, and I wish to welcome our witnesses and express my gratitude to them for taking time to come here, offer their personal experiences and insight.

The abuse of synthetic drugs, or designer drugs, has been recognized as far back as the 1980's. Producers of these drugs work continuously to create legal alternatives to controlled substances like marijuana, cocaine, ecstasy, LSD, and opioids that produce similar kinds of highs. Sometimes packaged in small, shiny packets with images of cartoon characters printed on them, and names like K2, Spice, Vanilla Sky, and Scooby Snax, these products are marketed as a harmless good time. Unsuspecting teenagers and young adults, who are the primary consumers of these products, can purchase so-called synthetic marijuana or bath salts at gas stations, convenience stores, novelty shops, and over the Internet for further reinforcing the erroneous belief that these products are safe.

However, in many cases, they are more potent and more hazardous than the controlled substances that they are meant to imitate. The chemical used to create synthetic drugs can be toxic to the human body, producing extreme paranoia, violent behavior, aggression, hallucinations, seizures, and even death. Synthetic drug use has even been linked to heart attacks, psychosis, and suicides. Instead of attending their child's football game or graduation or helping them complete college applications, parents find themselves in hospital rooms praying their teenager wakes from a coma or in emergency rooms hoping their child will regain their sanity and return to college.

There are mechanisms in current law to allow for these drugs to be evaluated and controlled on a case-by-case basis. For instance, the DEA has the ability to temporarily place substances on Schedule I, when it is necessary to avoid an imminent hazard to public safety.

However, the DEA is finding it difficult to keep pace with the development and production of new substances that are not currently illegal. Prosecutors have an additional tool, the Analog Enforcement Act of 1986, to prosecute those who produce synthetic drugs. This legislation serves as a method of criminalizing synthetic drugs without having to ban them individually. We in Congress need to learn more about these drugs and that is why this hearing is important, and consider if legislation is needed. And we must be careful to craft an appropriate response that does not over-criminalize or over-penalize. I thank our witnesses for their time and the benefit of their expertise.

I look forward to a discussion of this troubling issue. I thank the Chairman, and yield back.

Mr. BUCK. Thank you, Mr. Conyers. I would now like to recognize the full Committee Chairman, Mr. Goodlatte of Virginia, for his opening statement.

Mr. GOODLATTE. Thank you, Mr. Chairman. I am pleased to be here today as the Judiciary Committee continues its efforts to protect the American people from the real and growing danger of drug abuse. Last week, this Committee moved five bills through the House that will help law enforcement and the treatment community address the opioid epidemic, so this hearing is very timely. I want to focus my remarks today on the threat of synthetic opioids which present a critical threat to the American people.

As we all know, the principle driver of the opioid epidemic in this Nation has been the overabundance of prescription pain pills in the hands of consumers, especially opioids like oxycodone and hydrocodone. America's addiction to opioids has, of course, been noticed in the criminal underworld, and malefactors have taken big steps to profit off America's pain.

One way they have done this is through the production of synthetic opioids, including counterfeit prescription medications laced with fentanyl and fentanyl derivatives. For those who have been paying attention to this Committee's work, fentanyl is an opioid pain medication which can be 100 times more powerful than morphine.

To put that into perspective, Heroin is typically three times as powerful as morphine. Fentanyl is intended to be used to treat extreme pain associated with late stage cancer and other significant health problems. It is not intended to be used recreationally, yet it is, and with the rise of synthetic opioids, it is increasingly being used unknowingly.

Often drug traffickers will cut heroin with fentanyl to produce a more potent high. That has led to a rash of deaths across the country because of fentanyl's potency. In recent legislation, this Committee included language to provide for a sentencing enhancement for any offender who traffics in heroin cut with fentanyl.

With respect to synthetic opioids, fentanyl is also widely used. The profit margin is shocking. Less than a milligram of fentanyl can be lethal. That means a kilogram of fentanyl can generate enormous profits for the illicit trafficker, sometimes upward of a million dollars, so we have a problem. Between 2013 and 2014, the rate of drug overdose deaths involving synthetic opioids nearly doubled. According to the Centers for Disease Control and Prevention, a substantial portion of this increase appears to be related to the availability of illicit fentanyl.

According to the DEA's 2015 National Drug Threat Assessment, Mexico is the primary source country for illicitly produced fentanyl in the United States. However, pharmaceutical fentanyl has also been diverted from the legitimate supply chain and into the illicit market. Some derivatives and analogs of fentanyl are manufactured in China and shipped to the United States. Drug traffickers and associated profiteers are continuously developing new ways to exploit the American market. Evidence of new opioid drugs, some more powerful than fentanyl, are turning up on the American street corners.

For example, W18, a synthetic opioid potentially 100 times more powerful than fentanyl, which law enforcement has called the next deadly synthetic street drug. We are under siege. It is time for Congress to act, and this hearing represents a good first step. I thank the witnesses for their testimony, and look forward to the responses to our questions.

Mr. BUCK. I thank the Chair. Without objection, other Member's opening statements can be made part of the record.

Mr. GOODLATTE. Thank you, sir. I appreciate that very much.

Mr. BUCK. We have a very distinguished panel today. I will begin by swearing in our witnesses before introducing them. If you would all please rise. Raise your right hand.

Do you swear that the testimony you are about to give is the truth, the whole truth, and nothing but the truth, so help you God? Thank you, you may be seated.

Let the record reflect that all of the witnesses responded in the affirmative. Mr. Louis Milione, is that correct?

Mr. MILIONE. Yes.

Mr. BUCK. Special Agent Louis Milione is a deputy assistant administrator for the United States Drug Enforcement Administration's Office of Diversion Control, where he has served since October 2015. Mr. Milione acts as the principle advisor to the DEA administrator on matters pertaining to the regulation of programs relating to the diversion of legally produced controlled substances and listed chemicals. Mr. Milione began his career with the Drug Enforcement Administration in 1997, and holds a Bachelor of Arts degree from Villanova University, and a law degree from Rutgers University School of Law.

Officer William Smith, Jr., is an officer with the Washington, D.C. Metropolitan Police Department. He has over 20 years of law enforcement experience, much of which has focused on narcotics.

Mr. Devin Eckhardt is the father of Connor Eckhardt, who died tragically after smoking synthetic marijuana. Mr. Eckhardt is the founder of the Connor Project, and has addressed the United Nations to raise awareness globally about the dangers of synthetic drug use. He joins us today along with his wife, Veronica, in continuation of that effort.

Mr. David Nichols currently serves as an adjunct professor of chemical biology and medicinal chemistry at the University of North Carolina at Chapel Hill. He has been recognized as a distinguished professor emeritus at Perdue University, and as an adjunct professor emeritus of pharmacology and toxicology at Indiana University.

Dr. Nichols holds a Bachelor of Science degree in chemistry from the University of Cincinnati, a PhD in medicinal chemistry from the University of Iowa, and was a post-doctoral fellow in pharmacology at the University of Iowa.

We will now proceed. I will now recognize each of the witnesses for their opening statement, which will be limited to 5 minutes. Mr. Milione?

TESTIMONY OF LOUIS J. MILIONE, DEPUTY ASSISTANT ADMINISTRATOR, OFFICE OF DIVERSION CONTROL, DRUG ENFORCEMENT ADMINISTRATION

Mr. MILIONE. Thank you, Congressman Buck, distinguished Members of the Committee. Synthetic cannabinoids, synthetic cathinones, deadly fentanyl analogs, and other toxic synthetic substances are flooding the United States, putting unsuspecting users at risk of death and permanent injury. DEA sees this drug threat as second only to the opioid scourge that is currently devastating our country. Synthetic cannabinoids and cathinones are unpredictable, untested substances placed in colorfully market packaging and then marketed to our country's use as a legal high.

Emergency room doctors report a wide range of life-threatening side effects, including brain damage, cardiac arrest, kidney failure, and extreme psychosis. Synthetic cannabinoids and cathinones are sold openly in gas stations, convenience stores, head shops, and over the Internet from domestic and foreign sources.

Fentanyl analogs are a fast growing, particularly troubling part of this synthetic drug threat. Here you have the dangerous convergence of synthetic drugs with this country's opioid epidemic. With Fentanyl analogs, you have substances many times more potent than heroin that are being sold as heroin, mixed with heroin, or pressed into pill form and sold as prescription drugs. Fentanyl analogs are so deadly that a miniscule amount can kill an unsuspecting user. They can be ordered from Asia over the Internet and delivered directly to your home. Because of the massive profit potential, Mexican cartels are aggressively purchasing fentanyl and fentanyl analogs from Asia, shipping it into Mexico, mixing it with other substances, and distributing it throughout the United States. For all of us in the DEA, for all of our great Federal, State, and local law enforcement partners, for all the dedicated prosecutors around this country, our primary mission is to protect the public. In trying to protect the public from this synthetic drug threat, here is the most frustrating part. The foreign-based manufacturers and domestic pied pipers of this poison often operate with impunity because they exploit loopholes in the analog provisions of the Controlled Substances Act, and capitalize on the lengthy, resource intensive, reactive process required to schedule either permanently or temporarily these dangerous substances.

As we speak, criminal chemists in foreign countries are tweaking the molecular structure of controlled synthetics, keeping the same pharmacologic properties as the controlled substance, but helping the manufacturers and distributors avoid criminal exposure because of the altered molecular structure. We see these newly created synthetic drugs by the dozens every year. It is important to remember that these new dangerous substance get piled on top of the hundreds that we have already determined need to be controlled based on overdoses, deaths, and law enforcement encounters.

DEA moves to temporarily schedule as many of this growing backlog as quickly as we can, but for each substance that process averages between three and 4 months. Once temporarily scheduled, we seek HHS' evaluation for permanent scheduling, a process that can take at least several years for each substance.

Despite our best efforts, DEA cannot control these substances at a pace that will prevent additional overdoses and deaths. We at the DEA are very grateful for all the legislative and scheduling tools Congress has given us over the years. We have had success investigating, prosecuting, and convicting the traffickers of these dangerous substances using the Controlled Substances Act when the synthetic drugs are placed in Schedule I. We have also successfully used the Analog Act for substances not placed in Schedule I. However, today's synthetic drug crisis has outgrown the Analog Act. Thirty years ago, when the act was passed by Congress, there were far fewer analog users, and fewer traffickers than exist today. The trafficking networks that existed in 1986 were significantly less sophisticated than the transnational criminal networks currently operating.

We will continue to do everything we can, working with the tools you generously have given us to bring these substances under control and protect the public, but we are many steps behind the traffickers and need your help. In the short term, this esteemed body could provide DEA and our law enforcement partners throughout the country immediate relief by placing the hundreds of substances we have determined to be dangerous into Schedule I.

This would allow us to keep these synthetic drugs out of the country, get them off the shelves of retail stores, and bring to justice not the user population, but the egregious domestic and foreign traffickers preying on our youth, exploiting human frailty for profit, and flooding our country with these dangerous drugs. In the long term, we would welcome amendments to the Controlled Substances Analog Act that would align the act with the current threat, and/or perhaps other tools that would allow us to more quickly bring these drugs under control.

We stand ready to work with you, provide you any assistance we can, and address any of your concerns. One concern that has been raised is that placing hundreds of dangerous synthetic drugs into Schedule I will impede legitimate scientific research. Here are several facts that may inform that concern. DEA has never rejected a proposal for bona fide research with any Schedule I substance. Currently, there are 469 approved Schedule I researchers, and many have multiple approved protocols to study different Schedule I substances.

During the last year, it has taken an average of 32 days for DEA to approve a researcher's Schedule I application once that researcher has received FDA approval, a little more than 4 weeks. I would argue these are reasonable requirements when balanced with our duty to protect the public from these highly unstable and often deadly drugs. The DEA is committed to doing everything we can to address this threat. We look forward to working with Congress, with all our partners in the law enforcement, medical, and scientific communities to improve our effectiveness. Thank you very much for this opportunity, and I look forward to answering any questions you have.

[The prepared statement of Mr. Milione follows:]

 **Department of Justice**

STATEMENT OF

LOUIS J. MILIONE
DEPUTY ASSISTANT ADMINISTRATOR
OFFICE OF DIVERSION CONTROL
DRUG ENFORCEMENT ADMINISTRATION

BEFORE THE

HOUSE JUDICIARY SUBCOMMITTEE
CRIME, TERRORISM, HOMELAND SECURITY, AND INVESTIGATIONS
U.S. HOUSE OF REPRESENTATIVES

FOR A HEARING ON

SYNTHETIC DRUGS

PRESENTED

MAY 17, 2016

Statement of Louis J. Milione
Deputy Assistant Administrator
Office of Diversion Control
Drug Enforcement Administration
Before the
House Judiciary Subcommittee
Crime, Terrorism, Homeland Security, and Investigations
U.S. House of Representatives
May 17, 2016

INTRODUCTION

Chairman Sensenbrenner, Ranking Member Jackson Lee, and Members of the Subcommittee: on behalf of the approximately 9,000 employees of the Drug Enforcement Administration (DEA), thank you for the opportunity to discuss the threat posed by dangerous synthetic drugs.

Synthetic designer drugs, also known as New Psychoactive Substances (NPS), refer to man-made substances designed to mimic the effects of known licit and illicit controlled substances; these substances are oftentimes unscheduled and unregulated. There are a variety of synthetic designer drugs, which are categorized based on the types of controlled substances they are intended to mimic: cannabinoids, cathinones, and hallucinogens known as phenethylamines. The two most commonly used categories of synthetic designer drugs in the United States are synthetic cannabinoids and synthetic cathinones.

DEA has become increasingly alarmed over the proliferation of illicit fentanyl and its derivatives, which have been added to heroin and also encountered as counterfeit tablets resembling controlled prescription drugs (CPDs). Fentanyl and fentanyl derivatives are potent synthetic opioids which present a serious risk of overdose and death by those who misuse these substances. The yearly market for illegal non-medical prescription pain relievers is over 11 million people, and if fentanyl is introduced into even a small portion of that overall market, there is a likelihood that overdoses will increase. In addition, this drug can be absorbed by the skin or inhaled, which makes it particularly dangerous for public safety personnel who encounter the substance during the course of their daily operations. Fentanyl and fentanyl derivatives represent the deadly convergence of the synthetic drug threat and current national opioid epidemic.

SYNTHETIC DESIGNER DRUGS OVERVIEW

NPS represent the most recent area of concern for DEA. NPS are dangerous chemical compounds with no known legitimate medical or industrial use, and are not approved by the Food and Drug Administration (FDA) for use in medicine. These compounds pose a great danger to the public, especially children and teenagers, because they are falsely perceived as "legal" alternatives to the illicit drugs they intend to mimic and because of their unpredictable health impacts.

Synthetic Cannabinoids and Synthetic Cathinones

Synthetic cannabinoids and their products (sometimes sold under brand names such as K2 or Spice) continue to be a significant concern for public health and safety. These substances share biological activity with delta-9-tetrahydrocannabinol (THC), the primary psychoactive constituent in marijuana and are sourced from chemical manufacturers and suppliers primarily in China. Synthetic cannabinoid substances are typically prepared for packaging in the United States, and marketed over the Internet, or supplied to retail distributors before being sold to the public at retail stores (e.g., "head shops," convenience stores, gas stations, and liquor stores). Laws governing the legality of the substances vary widely between states and the chemical components are frequently altered, making it an on-going challenge for DEA to schedule these substances in a timely manner to protect the public.

Synthetic cathinones, also commonly known as "bath salts," can produce pharmacologic effects that are substantially similar to other controlled substances such as cathinone, methcathinone, MDMA, amphetamine, methamphetamine, and cocaine. In short, these substances are abused for their stimulant effects. These substances have been known to be marketed to consumers as "bath salts" or "glass cleaner." These substances are often labeled "not intended for human consumption" as a false means to defend against the Government's utilization of the federal Controlled Substance Analogue Enforcement Act (Analogue Act). Synthetic cathinones are widely available and have been encountered as a replacement for MDMA, a Schedule I controlled substance that is often referred to as "Molly."

NPS are a significant area of concern for DEA. According to the DEA National Forensic Laboratory Information System (NFLIS), substances identified as synthetic cannabinoids by federal, state, and local forensic laboratories increased from 23 reports in 2009 to 37,500 reports in 2014. Substances identified as synthetic cathinones increased from 29 reports in 2009 to 14,070 reports in 2014. This is the last full year for which data is available.

Synthetic cannabinoids and synthetic cathinones are almost entirely manufactured in China. They are then imported into the United States through mail services. Once in the United States, bulk powders are sprayed or otherwise applied on to plant matter and packaged into individual saleable units and then distributed for sale at gas stations, convenience stores, and head shops or sold directly to individuals via the Internet. Synthetic cathinones are usually snorted or swallowed in their powder or crystal forms. Side effects of synthetic cathinone use may include heart attack, kidney and liver failure, paranoia, panic attacks, and hyperthermia. Many drugs in this class are in Schedule I through legislative action or through administrative action to temporarily control the drug, initiated by DEA when the Administrator concludes that such action is necessary to avoid an imminent hazard to public safety. Unfortunately, when DEA initiates temporary control of a synthetic designer drug, those who traffic them frequently alter the chemical composition of the drugs they produce. These new substances, like the original substance, have an unpredictable impact on the body and pose a potentially severe public health threat.

NPS are typically used by younger individuals. Synthetic cannabinoids and synthetic cathinones are sold in packages adorned with bright colors and cartoons to attract younger users.

These drugs are often marketed under varieties such as blueberry, strawberry, mango, and bubblegum, to entice consumption.

Synthetic Opioids

Since 2014, DEA has encountered a dangerous new trend which represents the convergence of the synthetic drug threat and the epidemic of opioid abuse currently affecting our nation – clandestinely-manufactured fentanyl and fentanyl derivatives which are being added to heroin or replacing heroin altogether on the street. Fentanyl is a Schedule II controlled substance produced in the United States and used widely in medicine. It is an extremely potent analgesic widely used for anesthesia and also pain control in people with serious pain problems and in that case it is indicated only for use in people who are opioid tolerant.

DEA is increasingly encountering counterfeit prescription drugs laced with fentanyl and fentanyl derivatives. The DEA NFLIS reported that there were 7,864 fentanyl exhibits tested by forensic laboratories across the country in 2014 (the latest year for which data is available); a 742 percent increase from the 934 fentanyl exhibits in 2013.[1] The products, purchased illicitly, bear markings consistent with authentic prescription pain relievers such as oxycodone and hydrocodone, which may lead an unsuspecting user to believe he or she is consuming a legitimate controlled prescription drug. These counterfeit products have been found to contain lethal doses of fentanyl or fentanyl derivatives and are responsible for some overdose death outbreaks. Determining if one of these fentanyl-laced counterfeit prescription pills contains fentanyl based on sight alone is impossible; the presence of fentanyl can only be detected upon laboratory testing.

Illicit fentanyl, fentanyl derivatives, and their immediate precursors are often produced in China. From China, these substances are shipped through mail carriers directly to the United States or alternatively shipped directly to transnational criminal organizations (TCOs) in Mexico and the Caribbean. Once there, fentanyl or its derivatives are prepared to be mixed into the U.S. heroin supply domestically, or pressed into a pill form, and then moved to the illicit U.S. market where demand for prescription opioids and heroin remains high. In some cases, traffickers have industrial pill presses shipped into the United States directly from China and operate fentanyl pill press mills domestically. Mexican TCOs have seized upon this business opportunity because of the profit potential of synthetic opioids, and have invested in growing their share of this market. Because of its low dosage range and potency, one kilogram of fentanyl purchased in China for $3,000 - $5,000 can generate upwards of $1.5 million in revenue on the illicit market.

The consequences of fentanyl misuse are often fatal and occur amongst a diverse user base. Over a two week period in late March and early April 2016, DEA issued a public safety alert for the Sacramento, California region following an outbreak of overdoses related to counterfeit hydrocodone which had been laced with fentanyl. In all, there were 52 individuals who overdosed, with 14 of those ultimately losing their lives.

---

[1] (U) U.S. Department of Justice, Drug Enforcement Administration, National Forensic Laboratory Information System, Annual Reports 2004-2014.

In 2014, over 4.3 million Americans age 12 or older reported using prescription pain relievers non-medically within the past month. This makes nonmedical prescription opioid use more common than use of any category of illicit drug in the United States except for marijuana. The illicit market for prescription drugs is considerable in size, which significantly increases the risk that fentanyl or fentanyl derivative-laced counterfeit pills will cause more overdoses across the nation as they are more readily produced by drug trafficking organizations.

Law enforcement throughout the United States has been encountering fentanyl at historic levels. In 2014, the DEA NFLIS reported 7,864 instances where fentanyl was tested by forensic laboratories nationwide. This is five times as many fentanyl exhibits than what was submitted during the 2006 fentanyl crisis, and is a 742 percent increase from 2013. With fentanyl and its derivatives continuing to reach a greater share of this multimillion person illicit prescription drug market, there is the potential for a sharp increase in overdoses across the nation in the near term.

CURRENT CHALLENGES

Traffickers Adapting to the Law

Even though many NPS compounds have been controlled in Schedule 1 (the most highly controlled drugs, which for most purposes are equivalent to a ban) through temporary scheduling or by legislative or administrative scheduling (per 21 U.S.C. sections 811 and 812), entrepreneurs procure new synthetic cannabinoid compounds with relative ease. Clandestine chemists can easily continue to provide retailers with "legal" products by developing/synthesizing new synthetic cannabinoid products that do not appear on any schedule of controlled substances. In fact, when DEA takes an action to temporarily schedule a substance, retailers begin selling new versions of their products with new, unregulated compounds in them. In addition, these same retailers are provided with spurious chemical analyses that purport to document that the new product line did not contain any controlled substance.

Over the past several years, DEA has identified hundreds of designer drugs from at least eight different drug classes, the vast majority of which are manufactured in China. There are a seemingly infinite number of possible new chemical compounds that are on the horizon. Manufacturers and distributors will continue to stay one step ahead of any state or federal drug-specific banning or control action by introducing and repackaging new synthetic cannabinoid products that are not listed as such in any of the controlled substance schedules.

There is also a large financial incentive that continues to drive the wholesale and retail distribution of these products. Information that DEA has obtained through the course of its investigations demonstrate that a $1,500 purchase of a bulk synthetic cannabinoid can generate as much as $250,000 of revenue at the retail level. It is clear that the income generated from distributing these products is, and will continue to be, a driving factor for manufacturers, distributors, and retailers to seek and find substitute products that are not yet controlled or banned by federal or state action.

Prosecutions Pursuant to the Analogue Act

A designer drug may be a "controlled substance analogue" pursuant to the Controlled Substances Act (CSA) if it meets the criteria of substantial similarity of chemical structure and effect on the central nervous system. Even if a particular substance is widely regarded as a "controlled substance analogue" under the CSA, each criminal prosecution must establish that fact anew. The primary challenge to preventing the distribution and abuse of a controlled substance analogue, as opposed to a controlled substance *per se*, is that the latter is specifically identified (by statute or regulation) as a controlled substance to which clear statutory controls automatically attach, while the former is not specifically identified (by statute or regulation) and is treated as a Schedule I controlled substance only once proven to meet the definition of a controlled substance analogue; prosecutors must also prove that the substance was intended for human consumption. Accordingly, each prosecution is a new case even if the same substance is involved.

In addition, without establishment and inclusion of specific sentencing equivalencies in the U.S. Sentencing Guidelines, prosecutors are required to produce evidence addressing the factors identified in the relevant guidelines. This typically results in prosecutors calling two expert witnesses to testify at every sentencing hearing to demonstrate that the substances in question fall within guideline definitions, a time consuming, resource intensive, and inefficient process. Different courts have reached very different results for the same substance which has resulted in disparate sentences for similarly situated offenders.

The above considerations, along with the increasing volume and variety of designer drugs available today and the sophisticated methods and routes of distribution, render the Analogue Act a cumbersome and resource-intensive, tool to prevent manufacturing, trafficking, and abuse of designer drugs. That said, agents, chemists, and prosecutors have worked together tirelessly to make the Analogue Act work, with many successful prosecutions to show for it. The Synthetic Drug Abuse Prevention Act of 2012 (SDAPA) approach to control specific, known, synthetic substances in some instances by description of chemical characteristics, was a swift and aggressive contribution to the overall effort to combat the designer drug threat.[2] DEA will continue to identify ways to better combat the designer drug threat.

Lack of Scientific Evidence to Support Control

The CSA provides the Attorney General (delegated to the DEA Administrator) with a mechanism to bring new drugs of abuse under CSA control and subject them to a regulatory scheme to protect the public. This process is an interagency process and determinations about placement in the CSA are dictated by the following eight enumerated scientific factors:[3] the state of current scientific knowledge about the substance; its pharmacological effect; its risk to the public health; its psychic or psychological dependence liability; whether the substance is an immediate precursor of a controlled substance; its actual or relative potential for abuse; its

---

[2] P.L. 112-144 – Food and Drug Administration Safety and Innovation Act, Subtitle D, Section 1151, titled "Synthetic Drug Abuse and Prevention Act of 2012.

[3] The 8 factors are enumerated in 21 U.S.C. § 811(c).

history or current pattern of abuse and its scope; and the scope, duration, and significance of abuse. In this process, the Secretary for the Department of Health and Human Services (HHS) is responsible for any scientific and medical considerations about a substance and a recommendation made by the Secretary is considered by the DEA Administrator along with other relevant facts to determine whether there is substantial evidence to warrant control.

In circumstances when the DEA Administrator concludes that control of a substance is necessary to avoid an "imminent hazard to public safety," the DEA Administrator may initiate temporary control of that substance for a period of two years, subject to possible extension for up to one year,[4] during which time the interagency conducts the abovementioned scientific review for permanent placement under the CSA.[5]

DEA believes a coordinated response by public health and law enforcement and other stakeholders remains the most effective response to this problem. Earlier this year, scientific staffs from the FDA, the National Institute on Drug Abuse (NIDA), and DEA participated in discussions regarding a sampling of new psychoactive substances which were encountered on the illicit market and share similarity with controlled substances.[6] Often, the lack of scientific information for the new and rapidly emerging substances being encountered by law enforcement represents a significant challenge for DEA and other agencies as we seek to address this public health and safety threat. DEA continues to work with partners such as NIDA to collect pharmacological information critical to the evaluation of a number of synthetic designer drug substances for consideration for both temporary and permanent scheduling. Further, DEA will continue to share information and engage stakeholders to decrease the demand for NPS.

DEA RESPONSE TO THE THREAT OF SYNTHETIC DRUGS

Scheduling by Administrative Rulemaking: Temporary Control

DEA continues to utilize its regulatory authority to place many synthetic cannabinoids and synthetic stimulants into the CSA pursuant to the aforementioned temporary scheduling authority. Once a substance is temporarily placed in Schedule I, DEA moves towards permanent control by requesting a scientific and medical evaluation and scheduling recommendation from HHS and gathering and analyzing additional scientific data and other information collected from all sources, including poison control centers, hospitals, medical examiners, treatment professionals, and law enforcement agencies, in order to consider the additional factors warranting its permanent control. Since March 2011, DEA has utilized this authority on ten occasions to place 35 synthetic designer drugs into Schedule I, including two fentanyl analogues, butyryl fentanyl and beta-hydroxythiofentanyl. In comparison, over the first 25 years (1985-2010) after Congress created this authority, DEA utilized it a total of 13 times to control 25 substances.

---

[4] The temporary control of a substance is enumerated in 21 U.S.C. § 811(h).

[5] Temporary control of a substance may be extended for a period of 1 year if DEA receives the Secretary's scientific and medical evaluation and scheduling recommendation within the 2-year temporary control period.

[6] This review was undertaken for the substances named in HR 3537, introduced by Representative Charles Dent.

Recent Major Enforcement Operations

DEA's Operation Log Jam was initiated in 2011 and culminated in a nationwide takedown on July 25, 2012. This DEA Special Operations Division Operation resulted in multiple Organized Crime Drug Enforcement Task Forces (OCDETF) Operations throughout the United States, including those in 25 federal districts. This operation was coordinated by DEA in cooperation with U.S. Immigration and Customs Enforcement's Homeland Security Investigations (HSI), the Federal Bureau of Investigations (FBI), U.S. Customs and Border Protection (CBP), and the Internal Revenue Service (IRS). The goals of this operation included the targeting of manufacturers, wholesale distributors, and retail distributors of designer drug products, the development of information on foreign based sources of supply, raising public awareness of the dangers associated with the use of these drugs, and the development of leads for a Phase II initiative (Project Synergy).

Operation Log Jam resulted in 100 arrests; the execution of 300 search warrants and 80 consent searches, and the identification of 38 manufacturing sites. Law enforcement seized 196 kilograms of raw synthetic cathinones, 722 kilograms of raw synthetic cannabinoids, 167,187 packets of synthetic cathinones ready for distribution, 4,852,099 packets of synthetic cannabinoids ready for distribution, 4,766 kilograms of plant material treated with synthetic cannabinoids ready to be packaged, 21,933 kilograms of untreated plant material, over $45,000,000 in U.S. currency and bank accounts, 88 vehicles, 77 firearms, additional assets valued at $5,688,500, and 1,096 gallons of acetone.

The information and evidence obtained during Operation Log Jam led investigators to initiate Project Synergy, the second phase of a national cooperative effort in combating the synthetic designer drug distribution, which also resulted in multiple OCDETF operations in at least 13 federal districts. Project Synergy began in December 2012 and culminated in a nationwide take down on June 26, 2013 conducted by DEA, HSI, FBI, CBP, and the IRS, as well as domestic law enforcement departments in 45 states. This operation also included some of our international partners with joint operations being conducted with Australia, New Zealand, Canada, and Barbados.

As part of Project Synergy, DEA conducted an enforcement operation in June 2013 in the Houston, Texas, area on a synthetic cannabinoid wholesale distributor who was selling AM-2201 and XLR11. During this operation, law enforcement seized enough synthetic cannabinoid products to gross approximately $21,000,000 in revenue at the retail level.

Project Synergy involved many investigations that culminated on June 26, 2013, and included 234 arrests, 416 search warrants, and 68 consent searches that led to the seizure of 305 kilograms of raw synthetic cathinones; 1,278 kilograms of raw synthetic cannabinoids; 10,263 packets of synthetic cathinones and cannabinoids; 959 kilograms of treated plant material ready to be packaged; and $53,201,595 in currency and assets, 132 vehicles, and 141 weapons.

The second phase of Project Synergy culminated in May 2014 and involved law enforcement action in 29 states. More than 150 individuals were arrested and federal, state, and local law enforcement authorities seized hundreds of thousands of individually packaged, ready to sell synthetic drugs as well as hundreds of kilograms of raw synthetic products to make thousands more. More than $20 million in cash and assets were seized.

The third phase of Project Synergy which took place over 15 months and concluded in October 2015, was a collaborative effort between DEA, HSI, and CBP, along with other federal, state, and local law enforcement. This effort targeted the synthetic designer drug industry, including wholesalers, money launderers, and other criminal facilitators. It resulted in 151 arrests in 16 states and over $15 million seized in cash and assets. In addition to curbing the flow of synthetic drugs into the country, Project Synergy III continued to reveal the flow of millions of dollars in U.S. synthetic drug proceeds to countries in the Middle East.

Lastly, in September 2015, the DEA coordinated Operation Spice in partnership with the OCDETF New York Strike Force and multiple other law enforcement agencies in New York City in September. This massive takedown targeted the local sale of dangerous designer synthetic drugs manufactured in China. The scheme, which operated in all five boroughs of New York City, allegedly involved the unlawful importation of at least 100 kilograms of illegal synthetic compounds, an amount sufficient to produce approximately 1,300 kilograms of dried product, or approximately 260,000 retail packets. As part the operation, five processing facilities were searched, as well as warehouses used to process, store, and distribute the drugs. In addition, over 80 stores and bodegas around New York City were searched. Over two million packets of synthetic drugs were seized. These packets were ready for street distribution, concealed in over 100 laundry bags, and ready for delivery.

China: Government Action and Cooperation

Through both DEA leadership and its country office in Beijing, DEA has maintained an ongoing relationship with People's Republic of China Government Officials for years, and has been able to leverage this relationship to combat the rising threat from NPS. Engagement has been occurring at the leadership level through interagency working groups that operate under the U.S.-China Joint Liaison Group framework: the Counternarcotics Working Group led by the Department of Justice, and the Bilateral Intelligence Working Group led by DEA. Last October, China decided to implement domestic controls on 116 NPS, which included fentanyl derivatives. The United States, through DEA, is working with China to identify NPS as traffickers develop new ones, and China has streamlined its processes for scheduling additional NPS when identified. Finally, as this threat has increased, law enforcement cooperation at case level has been very productive, particularly on fentanyl cases. DEA will continue to collaborate with the Government of the People's Republic of China as the threat from NPS continues to evolve.

CONCLUSION

Synthetic cannabinoids, cathinones, opioids, and phenethylamines will continue to pose a nation-wide threat. Synthetic drug producers modify and experiment with chemical formulas in search of new psychoactive substances. Once a new drug is formulated, the Internet and social media are used to market its arrival on the scene, allowing for its fast adoption and use. Due to the changing nature of the chemical formula for synthetic designer drugs, distributors are able to reap significant profits before legislation to control these specific psychoactive substances is enacted. While synthetic drugs will remain prevalent as a whole, synthetic cannabinoid use will remain steady or increase, while synthetic cathinone use appears to be on the decline. The United States will continue to see overdoses and deaths as a result of synthetic drug use, primarily among the youth population.

Additionally, the United States continues to be affected by a national opioid epidemic, which has been spurred, in part, by the rise of nonmedical prescription opioid use and the large numbers of people with active substance use disorders who are not currently in treatment. It is likely that this demand will continue to be met in part by counterfeit prescription opioids which are being laced with fentanyl or fentanyl derivatives, and Mexican-based TCOs who are pushing to expand their profits. DEA will continue to address this threat by pursuing the Mexican-based TCOs which have brought tremendous harm to our communities. Additionally, DEA's Office of Diversion Control will use all criminal and regulatory tools possible to identify, target, disrupt, and dismantle individuals and organizations responsible for the illicit distribution of pharmaceutical controlled substances in violation of the CSA. We look forward to continuing to work with Congress to find legislative solutions needed to address the threat posed by synthetic drugs.

Mr. BUCK. Thank you, Special Agent Milione.

Mr. MILIONE. Thank you.

Mr. BUCK. Officer William Smith, I recognize you for 5 minutes.

Mr. SMITH. Good morning Mr. Chairman, distinguished Members of the Subcommittee on Crime, Terrorism, Homeland Security Investigations.

Mr. BUCK. Would you pull the microphone closer please? I am sorry to interrupt you. Would you pull the microphone a little closer to you?

TESTIMONY OF WILLIAM SMITH, JR., FRATERNAL ORDER OF POLICE

Mr. SMITH. I apologize. As first responders who respond to the individuals under the influence of synthetic drugs, the side effects of synthetic drugs are very common and similar to another drug which law enforcement officers encounter, which is phencyclidine, or PCP. As the Committee can see, I am not a small officer, and have dealt with individuals both underneath these synthetic drugs and PCP. And let it be known, even at my stature at times, it has been very difficult for myself and other officers to restrain these individuals.

Individuals under the influence of these substances have an absolute almost supernatural human strength and de-increased pain tolerance, which can lead to officers and other first responders being injured when dealing with these individuals. According to the Drug Enforcement Administration, poison control has seen a 229 percent spike in calls in relationship to synthetic drugs.

Hundreds of these synthetic drugs are manufactured overseas in China and Mexico with no regulations or medical purposes. There has been reported 49,000 new chemicals used in these synthetic drugs. This is costing children and teenagers their lives. Also, these synthetic drugs are designed to keep law enforcement from finding the origin of the chemicals. The DEA testified this past fall, in front of the House Energy and Commerce Committee, that they are three steps behind the criminals when it comes to synthetics and analogs. In the past few years, synthetic marijuana has become the popular choice for synthetic drugs. It is designed to mimic the effects of organic marijuana, and has a wide commercial availability. It can be bought at local stores for as little as $5 apiece, which made it popular among young people and the homeless.

This is because it is sold under interesting brand names, such as Bizarro, K2, Spice, and Scooby Snax. These synthetic drugs are usually manufactured in foreign facilities in China and Mexico, with an ever changing chemical cocktail. All 50 states have outlawed synthetic drugs in some way. The problem is that the ever changing chemical makeup. The manufacturers of these synthetic drugs keep changing the chemical makeup to try to skirt the law and claim that their product are not illegal.

Synthetic marijuana has two to five times the strength, amount of THC than normal marijuana, and the availability and high use of drugs in recent years have led to a 1400 percent increase in hospital visits from 2009 to 2012. Commissioner William Bratton of the city of New York Police Department stated, "This is the scourge on our society, affecting the most disadvantaged neighborhoods, our most challenged citizens.

It affects teenagers of public housing, homeless city shelters, and is quite literally flooding our streets." In the previous session of Congress, the FOP supported legislation to add synthetic bath salts, marijuana, and other synthetic drugs to DEA's schedule of controlled substance, but the chemical manufacturers have found loopholes for manufacturing and distributing these drugs, or analog drugs, because they are similar, but not chemically identical to the scheduled substances. With the loopholes, these manufacturers and distributors sell; and abusers of these synthetic substance all know exactly what to do with them. They ingest them, snort them to get a dangerous and unpredictable high.

In the past few years, we have found even more—seen more new drug of fentanyl. The synthetic fentanyl used by doctors is the most powerful opioids in medicine. However according to DEA, much of what is being found on the street is not diverted from hospitals, but rather sourced from China and Mexico. Frequently people buy it on the street with no idea it is fentanyl.

It is reported to be 100 to 200 times stronger than heroin. Just a quarter of a gram or a milligram, .25 milligrams, can kill you. To put it in perspective, just how little .25 milligrams is, a typical baby aspirin is 81 milligrams. If you cut that 81 milligram tablet into 324 pieces, one of these pieces would be equivalent to a quarter milligram. Admitting [spelled phonetically] the 80 percent of all fentanyl seizures in 2014 were concentrated in just 10 states: Ohio, Massachusetts, Pennsylvania, Maryland, New Jersey, Kentucky, Virginia, Florida, New Hampshire, and Indiana. I would like to thank the Committee for hearing our national FOP representation.

[The prepared statement of Mr. Smith follows:]

NATIONAL
FRATERNAL ORDER OF POLICE®

328 MASSACHUSETTS AVE., N.E.
WASHINGTON, DC 20002
PHONE 202-547-8189 • FAX 202-547-8190

CHUCK CANTERBURY
NATIONAL PRESIDENT

JAMES O. PASCO, JR.
EXECUTIVE DIRECTOR

TESTIMONY

Of

William Smith, Jr.

Fraternal Order of Police

on

"Dangers of Synthetic Drugs"

Before the

Subcommittee on Crime, Terrorism, Homeland Security, and

Investigations

— BUILDING ON A PROUD TRADITION —

Good morning, Mr. Chairman and the distinguished members of the Subcommittee on Crime, Terrorism, Homeland Security, and Investigations. I would like to thank Chairman Sensenbrenner for inviting the FOP to share the views of the 330,000 members of the Fraternal Order of Police on synthetic drugs, and I would like to thank Chuck Canterbury, National President, for asking me to represent the FOP.

Before I begin my remarks, I would like to thank Representative Dent for introducing H.R. 3537, the "Synthetic Drug Control Act," and Representative Katko for introducing H.R. 4229, the "Protecting Our Youth from Dangerous Synthetic Drugs Act." I would also like to thank the Chairman for his support on the Bulletproof Vest Partnership Grant. We are very grateful.

The abuse of synthetic drugs has become a major problem with increased reports from every region of the country indicating that individuals are committing violent acts while under the influence of these drugs. Many of these drugs induce elevated heart rates, increased blood pressure, and higher body temperature. They can also trigger seizures, hallucinations, and highly agitated states which make them very dangerous not just to the user but also for those around them, including Law Enforcement and other first responders, who respond to the aid of individuals under the influence of these synthetic drugs. The side effects of synthetic drugs are very similar to another drug which law enforcement officers encounter, Phencyclidine (PCP). As the Committee can see I am not a small officer and have dealt with individuals both under the influence of synthetic drugs and PCP. Let it been known, even at my stature, at times, has been difficult for myself and other officers to restrain those individuals. Individuals under the influence of these substances have an almost supernatural strength and increased pain tolerance which can lead to officers and other first responders being injured when dealing this individuals.

According to the Drug Enforcement Administration (DEA), Poison Control has seen a 229% spike in calls in relation to synthetic drugs. Hundreds of these synthetic drugs are manufactured overseas in China and Mexico with no regulation or medical purpose. There have also been reports of 49,000 new chemicals used in these synthetic drugs. This is costing children and teenagers their lives. Also, these synthetics are designed to keep law enforcement from finding the origin of the chemicals. The DEA testified this past fall in front of House Energy and Commerce Committee that they are "three steps behind" the criminals when it comes to synthetics and analogues.

In the past few years synthetic marijuana has become the popular choice of synthetic drugs. It is designed to mimic the effects of organic marijuana and has a wide commercial availability. It can be bought at local stores for $5, which has made it popular among young people and the homeless. That is because it is sold with interesting brand names such as Bizarro, K2, Spice, and Scooby Snax. These synthetic drugs are usually manufactured in foreign facilities, like China and Mexico, with an ever changing cocktail of chemicals. While all 50 states have outlawed synthetic drugs in some way, the problem is the ever changing chemical makeup. The manufacturers of these synthetics keep changing the chemical makeup of the drugs trying to skirt the laws and claim that their products aren't technically illegal.

Synthetic marijuana has 2-5 times the amount of THC in it than normal marijuana. The availability and high use of this drug in recent years has led to a 1400% increase in hospital visits from 2009-2012. Commissioner William Bratton of the City of New York Police Department said, "This is a scourge on our society, affecting the most disadvantaged neighborhoods and our most challenged citizens. It affects teenagers in public housing, homeless in the city shelter system, and it's quite literally flooding our streets."

In the previous session of Congress, the FOP supported legislation to add synthetic marijuana, bath salts, and other synthetic drugs to the DEA's Schedules of controlled substances, but the chemical manufacturers have found loopholes for manufacturing and distribution of these drugs or "analogue" drugs- because they are similar, but not chemically identical to the scheduled substances. With the loopholes these manufacturers, distributors, and sellers and abusers of these synthetic substances all know exactly what to do with them- ingest them or snort them to get a dangerous and unpredictable high.

In the past few years we have seen an even more dangerous new synthetic drug ravage our streets. This new drug is synthetic fentanyl. Used by doctors, fentanyl is the most powerful opioid in medicine. However, according to the DEA, much of what is being found on the streets is not diverted from hospitals but rather sourced from China and Mexico. Frequently, people buy it on the street with no idea that it is fentanyl.

It is reported to be between 100-200% stronger than heroin. Just a quarter of a milligram — 0.25 milligrams — can kill you. For a sense of just how little that is, a typical baby aspirin tablet is 81 mg.

If you cut that tablet into 324 pieces, one of those pieces would be equal to a quarter-milligram.

The week of April 4th saw 10 people die from drug overdoses that were caused by synthetic fentanyl. Several states have reported a surge in deaths caused by fentanyl. It is estimated that two thirds of the 420 overdose deaths in New Hampshire can be attributed to this synthetic drug. The vast majority of fentanyl use is attributed to heroin where it is used as a cutting agent to increase potency.

This year in California fentanyl was passed off as the prescription drug Norco and sold on the streets. In just one 10-day period, this batch was responsible for at least 10 deaths and 48 overdoses.

More than 80% of all fentanyl seizures in 2014 were concentrated in just 10 states: Ohio, Massachusetts, Pennsylvania, Maryland, New Jersey, Kentucky, Virginia, Florida, New Hampshire and Indiana.

In 2013, Ohio reported 92 fentanyl-related overdose deaths. The next year, there was a five-fold increase, with 514 deaths. In Maryland, the number of overdose deaths jumped from 58 in 2013 to 185 the next year.

The drug naloxone can reverse an opioid overdose. However, because fentanyl is so potent, it may require several doses of naloxone to bring someone out of a fentanyl overdose. That is why it is of particular concern when people don't know whether they are even using fentanyl have an overdose.

Law enforcement is in danger as well when dealing with synthetic fentanyl. The DEA stated that fentanyl is extremely dangerous even to law enforcement and anyone else who may come into contact with it, so the police tactics used to directly attack the drug trafficking networks producing and importing the drugs actually put the officers in danger when coming into contact with the substance, because it is so potent. In a video released by CNN, the DEA showed personal protective equipment (PPE) which police officers and DEA specialists need to use in order to handle the product without being exposed to health risks.

In the last few months an even more dangerous new synthetic drug from Canada has emerged with the street name W-18. W-18 was originally formulated and patented at the University of Alberta, Canada in 1984, the only testing of W-18 was on done on mice and no pharmaceutical company would touch it and the recipe sat on a shelf, until a Chinese chemist found it and he is believed to have started manufacturing it in China and selling it online. W-18 resurfaced in Canada last fall. This drug is 10,000 times more powerful than morphine and 100 times more powerful than fentanyl. W-18 has already been found in Pennsylvania and Florida. In March, a man in Florida was found to have two and a half pounds of W-18 when he was arrested for selling fentanyl pills; unfortunately the individual was only charged for smuggling fentanyl, as W-18 is not yet an illegal scheduled narcotic.

Research currently does not know if the lifesaving drug Naloxone for overdoses even has an effect on a drug like this. W-18 also looks just like heroin and cannot be differentiated by the human eye. There is no test to determine if an individual has introduced W-18 into their body and we do not know if this drug can be attributed to the recent spike in overdose deaths.

In conclusion, the FOP is ready to work with the Committee on the issue of synthetic drugs. There are many areas on this issue on which I expect there to be broad agreement. This is a public health, and a public safety crisis that is destroying our communities across the country and needs to be acted upon now.

Thank you for having me here today and I am pleased to answer any questions you might have.

————

Mr. BUCK. Thank you, Officer Smith. I now recognize Mr. Eckhardt. If you could turn your microphone on for 5 minutes. Thank you very much.

TESTIMONY OF DEVIN ECKHARDT, FOUNDER OF THE CONNOR PROJECT FOUNDATION

Mr. ECKHARDT. Before I begin, I would like to make sure that each of the Committee Members has a copy of the brochure. Thank you. As it was stated, my name is Devin Eckhardt, and I am joined by my wife Veronica. And for very personal reasons, we chose to join you here today as you dedicate some time to better understanding the threats and issues surrounding new psychoactive substances, sometimes referred to as synthetic designer drugs, the epidemic rate at which they are spreading, the severity of their destructive effects both within the U.S. and globally, and the deadly impact they are having upon our countries, our communities and our families.

And it is our sincere hope and prayer that each of you will leverage both your individual and collective power to do more than simply discuss this growing problem, but rather you will choose to take action now and make changes necessary to eradicate these deadly poisons and their proliferation. It is my hope that my testimony will help provide some heart to the head knowledge that you hear so frequently in these conversations.

Sadly my wife, family, and I tragically know all too well the devastating impact of synthetic drugs. In July of 2014, our 19 year old son Connor was a bright, vibrant young man with a full life ahead of him. He was really what most would have considered the all-American young boy. He had a great job. He was preparing to go back to college. He loved music, surfing, the outdoors. He had lots of friends, and of course he was deeply loved by his family, his sisters, his mother, and of course me, his father.

This first photo here was a family shot taken July 5th of 2014. It was the last time we would be together like this as a family. Eight days later, Connor was with a new friend. He made the seemingly innocent decision. He agreed to try something called Spice, a synthetic poison, and the result was the second photo there. After many days in the hospital with our son in a coma, he was ultimately declared brain dead. Connor died July 16th, 2014, after one smoke of a legal high purchased at a local store.

At the time, we were unaware of NPSs, and we made the decision to share our story publically, to be painfully transparent and naked with our tragedy before a watching world, with the simple hopes that perhaps it might change one person's life. It might spare them and their family the horrific circumstances that we were facing and that we now live with each day.

Since the death of our son 671 days ago, we have met far too many parents who have also lost their children to synthetic drugs like Spice. And through our outreach, speaking, and education efforts over these past 671 days, we have communicated with literally hundreds of thousands of people throughout the United States and around the world who have lost loved ones or had their lives tragically destroyed by synthetic drugs.

Unfortunately, what happened to Connor is not unique. Far too many people have suffered irreparable harm, including death, as a result of trying or using these poisons. However, what is unique about his story is how it is received an overwhelming global response to what we have shared publically through social media, news interviews, TV, radio broadcasts around the world. His story has cut through the racial, socioeconomic, geographic, and religious barriers typically encountered. We know that NPSs are affecting everyone everywhere. We are not just one voice. Connor is not just one face or some statistic. We represent the voice and the face of the many others just like us.

We have had the opportunity to reach millions of people on this subject. We have been interviewed by most of the major news and media outlets around the U.S. and globally, and of course we have leveraged social media. We have had individually unique Facebook posts that have reached millions at a time, with one reaching over 37 million people globally. We have had the opportunity to speak in many settings. We have worked with and spoken to senators, legislators, law enforcement officials, and many in government. We even met with a lord from the House of Lords in the U.K. this past summer as we were there on this subject.

We have worked with numerous organizations in an effort to educate and increase awareness on the dangers of synthetic drugs, and we have worked to change the laws so that these poisons are removed from our streets, our stores, and our communities, but more must be done. The problem is getting worse. Hundreds of new synthetic drug compounds have appeared around the world in the last few years, sometimes spreading at the rate of a new drug per week, and we are allowing these to come into our country.

Illicit drug manufacturers are constantly working and changing the formulas, developing new chemical derivatives in order to evade the laws, and frankly they are working faster than we are. The issue of NPSs needs to be addressed and it needs to be done now.

When this congressional gathering has ended, you return home. You will return to your families, your children, those you love and care for. When we return home, we return to a family that has been forever changed, because of the death of our beloved son as the result of synthetic drugs. As long as the people around the world pushing these poisons into our communities know that there are little or no consequence for their actions, and they do know this, we will continue to see the spread of synthetic drugs and the terrible harm they are bringing to our families, and to our youth and communities. You have the power to do something about this. You are in positions of influence and leadership, and we are pleading with you to please take action. Do not just talk about and debate the issues. Bring about change that will get these sub- stances out of our communities, and deal appropriately with those behind the manufacturing and distribution of NPSs globally. Thank for your time and your consideration on this.

[The prepared statement of Mr. Eckhardt follows:]

because every life matters
Awareness • Education • Prevention

Statement of Devin & Veronica Eckhardt
Parents of Connor Eckhardt
Founders of The Connor Project Foundation
Before the
House Judiciary Committee
United States Senate
May 17, 2016

Stats:

90	more than 90 countries have reported instances of New Psychoactive Substances (NPSs) in their country
11	percent of high school seniors in US that have tried or use NPSs
229	percent increase in phone calls to poison control centers across the US related to the use of synthetic drugs in the first half of 2015
9,000+	calls to poison centers in 2015 related to NPSs
300+	NPS compounds encountered by law enforcement in the US since 2009
277	people treated in Austin TX in for NPSs in June 2015
48,000	ED visits related to NPSs in 2011
15,796	ED visits of patients age 12-20 for NPSs in 2011
1	every single life matters... for every one person we help... it will make a difference to them, my son represents one of those statistical numbers
672	days since I last held my son; since his death

Good morning, Judiciary Subcommittee Members. My name is Devin Eckhardt and I am joined by my wife Veronica, and for very personal reasons we chose to join you here today as you dedicate some time to better understanding the threat and issues surrounding New Psychoactive Substances (sometimes referred to as synthetic designer drugs), the epidemic rate at which they are spreading, the severity of their destructive effects both within the USA and globally, the deadly impact they are having upon countries, our communities and our families.

We sincerely appreciate the opportunity to join you for this critically important conversation and it is our sincere hope and prayer that each of you will leverage your individual and

collective power to do more than simply discuss this issue, but rather, that you will choose to take action and make the changes necessary to eradicate these deadly poisons and their proliferation.

We want you to stop and reflect for a moment... how many of you have children of your own? Young children or grown, or perhaps grandchildren? Think about your family, your children, those who are deeply important to you.

We too have children. What we have learned after traveling around the country, around the world and spending time in many different countries, cultures and with many different nationalities is this... parents deeply love their children. They want the best for them and they are willing to do whatever it takes to care for their children and for their children's future. I'd be willing to bet that is true of each of you, and I know that is true for us.

You may be wondering about the numbers stated when I first started to speak... those are not just numbers. They represent the lives of people, children young and old who have been negatively impacted by NPSs.

REVIEW THE STATS ABOVE AGAIN

Sadly, my wife Veronica, our family and I tragically know all too well the devastating impact of these synthetic drugs.

In July of 2014, our 19 year old son Connor was a bright, vibrant young man with a full life ahead of him. He really was what most would have called the "All-American" young man. He was working, gaining promotions, preparing to go back to college, he loved music, surfing, the outdoors and was loved and adored by his many friends... and of course, he loved his family and was deeply loved by his sisters, his mother and by me, his father.

Here is a photo of our family – that's me, my wife Veronica, Connor, and our daughters Sabrina and little Ashnika who we adopted from Ethiopia. This was taken on the 5th of July 2014. This was the last time we'd be together like this as a family.

8 days later, Connor was with a new friend and made the <u>seemingly innocent decision</u> to try something called spice (an NPS)... and the result was this (photo). After many days in the hospital, our son was ultimately declared brain dead. Connor died July 16, 2014 after one smoke of spice.

At the time when this happened we, and obviously Connor, had never heard of the dangers of synthetic drugs or the proliferation of these deadly NPSs.

because every life matters
Awareness • Education • Prevention

We made the decision while still in the hospital with Connor to share our story publicly, to be painfully transparent, raw and naked with our tragedy before a watching world with the hopes that perhaps it might change one person's life and spare them and their family the horrific circumstances that we were facing and that we now live with each day.

Since the death of our son 672 days ago, we have met far too many parents who have also lost their children to synthetic drugs like Spice, and through our outreach, speaking and education efforts over these past 672 days, we have literally communicated with hundreds of thousands of people throughout the United States and around the world who have lost loved ones or had their lives destroyed by synthetic drugs.

Unfortunately, **what happened to Connor is not unique**. Far too many people have suffered irreparable harm, including death, as a result of trying or using NPSs. However, **what is unique about Connor's story** is how it has received an overwhelming global outcry in response to what we've shared publicly through social media, news, TV and radio broadcasts around the world. His story has cut through racial, socio-economic, geographic, and religious barriers typically encountered. What we know is that NPSs are affecting everyone, everywhere.

Thousands of young people are devastated each year with horrific side effects, including death, from synthetic drugs and the numbers continue to grow. Something must be done. Literally tens of millions of people around the world have read and shared our Facebook page since our tragedy struck. They tell us about how spice has taken hold of their lives, or lives of people they love; the pain and sorrow when someone ends up in a vegetative state or worse because of synthetic drug use; the choice to become sober and not to use any type of drugs; the hope they feel when they see the impact our story has had on their children.

What we have found out about synthetic drugs and their impact on our youth has shocked and dismayed us. It really is the deadliest and ugliest secret. We are losing a generation. We must do all we can to make sure synthetic drugs are eradicated. Our desire is that our kids, young adults and those that love them become educated about the significant dangers associated with synthetic drugs and have the tools necessary to resist this deceptively marketed seductive killer.

We have learned that Connor's story is a catalyst for change. The more we spread it, the more people reach out to us and tell us of their decision to change, to stop using, to never use and to help their friends. We may not be able to stop those using NPSs from exploiting and victimizing our children, but we can help our youth choose life and a future. We invite you to join us and help our youth live into the promise of a future free from synthetic drugs.

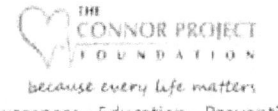

because every life matters
Awareness ▪ Education ▪ Prevention

We have had the opportunity to reach literally millions of people on this subject. We have been interviewed by most of the major news and media outlets including: The Today Show, FOX News, ABC, NBC, CBS, twice on BBC News, Daily Mail and of course Facebook.

Our individual unique Facebook posts have reached millions at a time with one post even reaching over 37 million people globally. We've heard from numerous countries around the world... the USA of course, Canada, countries throughout South America and across Africa, Europe, frequently from the UK, Ireland, Germany, Italy, Sweden, Russia, Japan, Australia, New Zealand... and many more.

We have had the opportunity to speak in schools, churches, youth groups, youth camps, community parent meetings... we've worked with and spoken to senators, legislators, many government officials, law enforcement officials... we even met with one of Lords from the House of Lords on this subject while we were in the UK this past summer.

We've worked with numerous organizations in an effort to educate and increase awareness on the dangers of synthetic drugs and have worked to change laws so that these poisons are removed from our streets, our stores, and our communities.

Something must be done, the problem is getting worse. This past November 2015 - IN ONE DAY ALONE - 13 people ranging from ages 13-45 were taken to San Diego emergency rooms due to the use of synthetic drugs. In May 2014, 15 people ended up at the emergency room due to NPSs. And then right in the city where I live, Sacramento CA, the week of March 21st we learned of 28 people who "over dosed" and 9 who died from synthetic fentanyl... and those numbers have continued to increase.

This is happening in towns, cities and countries all across the globe.

Poison control centers across the USA saw a 229% increase in phone calls related to the use of synthetic drugs in just the first half of 2015. The issue and problem of synthetic drugs is growing and something must be done, now.

The DEA here in the USA reports that hundreds of new synthetic drug compounds have appeared on the streets in the last few years, sometimes they experience as much as a new drug per week. We have spoken to emergency room doctors and nurses who have told us that they have seen an alarming increase in patients presenting with synthetic drug related symptoms – and because these drugs do not show up in a typical drug and alcohol test, medical professionals often just don't know what substances and chemical effects they are dealing with.

because every life matters
Awareness • Education • Prevention

There have been various legislative efforts to address the problem of NPSs by passing laws against the chemicals contained in them. And while these efforts are good, the problem is that the illicit drug manufacturers are constantly working and changing the formulas, developing new chemical derivatives & variants in order to evade the laws... and frankly they are working faster than we are; always seeming to stay a few steps ahead of the law.

Additionally, most of the legislative efforts are simply inadequate deterrents. I recognize that the larger issue of drugs, addiction, substance abuse which surround the specific issue of NPSs is complex and is not easily resolved through a new law. However, I believe that broader, stricter laws with more severe consequences are needed in order to deter the growing proliferation of NPSs across our country.

We need to collaboratively address the issue of NPSs and it needs to be done now. We need specific laws addressing the issues with consequences that will deter the sale, distribution and possession of any and all NPSs that are killing and permanently damaging our youth and adults.

When this Congressional gathering has ended and you return home... you will return to your families, to your children. When we return home... we return to our family that has been **forever changed** because of the death of our beloved son as a result of NPSs.

As long as the people around the world pushing these drugs into our communities know that there is little or no consequence for their actions, and they DO know this, we will continue to see the spread of NPSs and the terrible harm they are bringing to our families, our youth and our communities.

You have the power to do something to change this. You are in positions of influence and leadership. We are pleading with you to please take action. Don't just talk about and debate the issues. Bring about change that will get these substances out of our communities and will deal appropriately with those behind the manufacturing and distribution of NPSs globally.

We want to thank you for your time and consideration on this important issue. We are available if any of you have questions or would like to talk further.

Sincerely,
Devin and Veronica Eckhardt
Founders, The Connor Project Foundation

Mr. BUCK. Thank you, Mr. Eckhardt, thank you for your courage, and I appreciate your wife being here also. Thank you. Dr. Nichols, I recognize you for 5 minutes.

TESTIMONY OF DAVID EARL NICHOLS, Ph.D., ADJUNCT PROFESSOR OF CHEMICAL BIOLOGY AND MEDICINAL CHEMISTRY AT THE UNIVERSITY OF NORTH CAROLINA AT CHAPEL HILL

Mr. NICHOLS. Congressman Buck, is my microphone on? Congressman Buck, Members of the Committee, thank you for the opportunity to appear today. During my career, I worked with synthetic drugs, possessing a researcher's Schedule I DEA registration. My goal was to understand how the structure of a molecule engaged a biological target. Thus, better understanding how these substances act in the brain. I am very concerned about the potential harms to human health presented by synthetic drugs. Their availability requires a response, including regulation.

Yet I do not believe that the proposed legislation would have prevented the recent emergence of Spice mixtures. Rather they focus on already known controlled substance types. We badly need reasonable approaches to controlling new chemo types of synthetic substances. The challenge is to preserve researcher's needs while also stemming the flow of dangerous synthetic chemicals.

An appropriate response should consider three points. First, allowing research of potential therapeutic uses. Second, legislation should be guided by rigorous science. And third, the impact on mass incarceration, especially in cases where substances have not been fully vetted by the scientific community. Few investigators will pursue research with Schedule I drugs. Various researching Schedule I substances discourage engagement. Obtaining a Schedule I license is not a trivial matter, and a researcher must be very motivated to obtain one, even if the investigator requires only small drug amounts that do not represent a potential for diversion.

In most cases, researchers are funded, for example, by NIDA, to study only the deleterious properties of a specific drug of abuse. But it is also important to have funding available for research to identify beneficial properties of Schedule I substances, as with recent medical marijuana.

The costs and regulatory burdens of a Schedule I license deter research that might lead to new medicines. Research on Schedule I drugs is important, because in the last decade, clinical studies have indicated that psilocybin, a Schedule I drug, may have unique therapeutic efficacy in treating anxiety, depression and addiction to alcohol and nicotine.

As another example, Professor Charles Nichols at LSU decided to study the receptor targets of hallucinogens before he had a Schedule I license. The only hallucinogen available without a license was called DOI. He discovered, quite by accident, that DOI has potent anti-inflammatory properties, indicating potential efficacy in treating cardiovascular disease and asthma. Had DOI been a Schedule I, he never would have discovered this therapeutic breakthrough. Most pharmaceutical companies have a ban in research on novel drugs for depression, bipolar disorder, obsessive compulsive disorder, and others. They have unknown causes, the research is extremely expensive with a low probability of success. Ironically, the kinds of substances we are concerned with here today act in the brain, and it is quite possible that new medicines will result from more research on them. Any responsible legislation should protect research that might lead to the discovery of new medicines.

Without solid scientific evidence, it is unwise to schedule new molecules with untested potential. Sometimes changing a single atom on a molecule can dramatically alter its pharmacology. Superficial comparisons of chemical structure resemblance or predicted pharmacological effects, as in some proposed bills, are not a reliable basis for Schedule I classification. For example, bupropion or Wellbutrin, an effective anti-depressant, resembles Cathinone, yet it has no abuse potential.

There are hundreds of thousands of synthetic compounds that could be made, and we still know very little about just a few of the most recent ones. Also, there is no schedule category for drugs that have no known medical value, but which have also not been shown to have high abuse potential. We should carefully research compounds flagged by law enforcement by scheduling only those who have demonstrated public health and safety risks. Input from the scientific medical community would preclude the scheduling of compounds with no demonstrated public health dangers, preventing needless prosecution and incarceration of individuals for using these substances. Persons who manufacture and distribute these substances that harm human health should be held accountable.

But many people today do not believe that making users criminals for simple possession is appropriate. There is a consensus developing that use of psychoactive substances is a public health problem, not a criminal matter. The war on drugs has been largely unsuccessful in preventing drug use, and has contributed to our country having the largest prison population in the world, a large percentage of whom were incarcerated as a result of non-violent drug offenses.

In summary, the proliferation of new synthetic substances represents a great threat to the health of our youth. And regulation must be a component to the solution of this problem. But I strongly believe drug control and scheduling decisions should be grounded in the best science. There must be balance between the needs of research and enforcement, so that potential new therapeutic discoveries are not lost by restricting access to novel compounds. Humans and adolescents in particular, are known to be curious and to experiment. But most pass through that phase without serious consequences. Draconian penalties and felony convictions for use only add to the problem. Thank you.

[The prepared statement of Mr. Nichols follows:]

"Synthetic Drugs, Real Danger"

United States House of Representatives
Committee on the Judiciary
Subcommittee on Crime, Terrorism, Homeland Security, and Investigations

David Earl Nichols, PhD
Adjunct Professor of Chemical Biology and Medicinal Chemistry at the University of North
Carolina at Chapel Hill, NC
Former Robert C. and Charlotte P. Anderson Chair in Pharmacology and
Distinguished Professor of Medicinal Chemistry and Molecular Pharmacology
Purdue University College of Pharmacy, West Lafayette, IN
May 17, 2016

*The views expressed here are my own and not those of any institution with which I am now or have previously been affiliated.

Chairman Sensenbrenner, Ranking Member Jackson Lee, and Members of the Committee, thank you for the opportunity to appear today.

I wish to highlight three overarching themes in what I shall present. The first is that placing substances into Schedule 1 presents barriers to research and discovery of potential new therapeutics; second is that drug scheduling should be driven by the best science and evidence of actual abuse, and not guessing; and finally that in any new legislation we would hope to avoid creating schedules of compounds for which there is no evidence of harm to human health and leading to increasing the incidence of incarceration we have witnessed as a result of the drug war.

For most of my professional career, going back to my graduate training, I worked with a variety of what are now called synthetic drugs, and possessed a Researcher's Schedule 1 Drug Enforcement Administration (DEA) registration for many different kinds of abusable substances. My primary research goal was to understand how the structure of a molecule allowed it to engage a biological target, usually in the brain, which led to a better understanding of the brain mechanisms of action for these substances. I pursued significant research with psychostimulants such as substituted amphetamines, MDMA (ecstasy), and various hallucinogens, including LSD, mescaline, psilocybin, and numerous synthetic molecules. The type of work I did is called structure-activity relationship (SAR) studies, which requires working with a variety of different types of molecules to determine what structural elements they may have in common.

Let me state at the outset that I am very concerned about the potential harms to human health that can be presented by new "synthetic drugs". Sadly, I am acutely aware of the problem because some of my own research publications were mined by unscrupulous persons for illegal purposes and economic gain. It is very clear to me that the use and availability of these substances

requires some kind of response, including regulation. Yet, I have seen nothing in the proposed

legislation that would have prevented the recent rapid emergence of synthetic cannabimimetic

compounds, such as those incorporated into so-called Spice mixtures. Rather, the proposed

legislation is focused on expanding the chemical landscape around previously known controlled

substances. Considerable thought needs to be given to reasonable approaches to controlling

completely new chemotypes of synthetic substances, beyond those we already know about.

The real question is what the nature of that response should be, so that legitimate needs for

researchers can be preserved, while still being able to stem the flow of dangerous synthetic

chemicals. I believe that an appropriate response should include an examination of the following

three policy questions: first, what barriers to research examining potential therapeutic uses for a

substance will be created by scheduling that substance; second, how rigorously is science and

best evidence guiding the development of drug scheduling legislation and policy decisions on

this issue; and three, what impact will drug scheduling legislation and policy decisions on this

issue have on mass incarceration, especially in cases where substances that have not even been

fully vetted by the scientific community for possible dangers to human health (i.e. when we

don't know for certain that the substances proposed for scheduling will actually have abuse

potential or addiction liability) have been added to a drug schedule.

Drug Control Should Not Undermine Research

As an example, for about a decade I had a grant to study how MDMA worked in the brain, but a

secondary focus of my work was to identify possible new analogues of MDMA that might have

therapeutic potential. At a certain point it became clear that there was no interest in funding the latter type of research, but only in understanding why MDMA seemed to cause neurodegeneration in rodents. I ended my research on MDMA analogues at that point.

In my experience, when a compound is placed into Schedule 1, very few investigators are interested in pursuing research with it, except in certain specific instances. Barriers to researching Schedule 1 substances are a driving factor for this lack of engagement. Obtaining a Schedule 1 license is not a trivial matter. A researcher first of all has to have a reason or motivation to obtain the license. In most cases today it will be to study the deleterious properties of a specific drug of abuse, to understand how and why it negatively impacts the health of an individual. Federal institutes such as NIDA usually fund these studies, and many biomedical scientists follow these avenues of research.

By contrast, there is currently no Federal funding available for research that could identify *beneficial* properties of a Schedule 1 substance, with the possible exception of recent studies of medical marijuana. In these cases, the investigator must have a strong personal belief that something useful will be discovered by their research that is of sufficient importance to justify the regulatory demands of a Schedule 1 license. To wit, a researcher must submit an application to the DEA that includes the investigator's scientific credentials, the description of the laboratory, a precise description of the work to be carried out, listing the specific substance to be used, and a calculation of how much substance will be needed and for how long. If the DEA determines that the request for license is justified, there is then an inspection of the storage facility the investigator will use, to ensure that the controlled substance cannot be easily diverted, in some cases involving the purchase of a heavy safe by the investigator or their institution and/or enhanced security procedures. Inventory and use must be documented, and there is a license fee for most non-public institutions. In addition, unlike Schedules II-V of the CSA, a schedule 1 license must be obtained for a specific chemical entity. If an investigator wishes to work with additional Schedule 1 substances, a separate application or amended application must be submitted. All of these costs and regulatory burdens can be onerous, especially for academic investigators with lean research budgets.

These requirements are not waived or reduced if the investigator plans to use amounts of controlled substance that do not represent a significant potential for diversion. For example, mescaline is a hallucinogen with a human dose in the range of 200-400 mg. If an investigator wishes to carry out mouse studies with mescaline, they might typically require only 20-30 mg, much less than a single human dose. Yet, the Schedule 1 license application process and storage requirements remain the same as if the investigator was requesting to use several grams of the substance. That is not an extreme case, as many studies today can be carried out in cells, which might require only a few milligrams of a controlled substance. In the laboratory where I currently work, there is a large drug screening facility funded by the NIMH. Recently, the laboratory director was asked whether he could screen a large number of new synthetic substances, analogues that had recently been scheduled, but for which very little pharmacology was known. Even though such screening would involve only a few milligrams of each substance, he was forced to decline the request because he did not have a Schedule 1 license for each new compound that needed to be screened. That is an issue that certainly bears some consideration in developing any new legislation.

Pharmaceutical companies today often search for novel therapeutic actions in large, cell-based assays, generally referred to as High Throughput Screens (HTS). However, they generally will not include controlled substances or controlled substance analogues in their screening libraries because a license would be required to include each specific compound in the library, despite the fact that the amounts of controlled substances involved in HTS are miniscule.

Why is research involving Schedule I drugs so important? Let me begin answering this question by noting an area of historical interest that is relevant to the discussion here today. In the 1950s and 1960s there was widespread recreational use of hallucinogens such as LSD and psilocybin, ultimately leading to the Controlled Substances Act of 1970. Despite numerous anecdotal reports of therapeutic effects of these substances, the 1970 law led to a virtual cessation of all clinical research with LSD, psilocybin, or similar Schedule I substances. Yet, in the past decade, several small pilot and Phase 2 clinical studies have been completed both in the U.S. and in Europe, which indicate that psilocybin may have unique therapeutic efficacy in treating anxiety, depression, and addiction to alcohol and nicotine, after only one treatment.

If these early results can be confirmed in larger Phase 3 studies, it will be a major therapeutic advance for psychiatry in treating these, and other very difficult to manage conditions. These pilot and Phase 2 clinical studies were not supported by any government agency, but rather as a result of the personal commitment of a small number of scientists and clinicians who believed that early clinical studies of hallucinogens had been flawed, and that perhaps new and better designed clinical experiments might finally reveal whether hallucinogens actually possessed any medical benefit. Indeed, in 1993 I was a founder of a small not-for-profit research institute that supported these studies. In the absence of Federal agency support, a number of philanthropists became convinced by our rigorous approach to science that these studies were worthy of support. The committee will recognize that this approach took substantial personal commitment, as it ran counter to conventional wisdom and lacked access to significant institutional funding. In effect,

Schedule I designation has hindered this potential advance in medicine for more than four decades, and continues to hinder additional research.

As a second example, consider the case of 3,4-methylenedioxymethamphetamine (MDMA; ecstasy), a Schedule I drug. Commonly used at dance parties and raves worldwide for the past several decades, recent Phase 2 clinical studies have demonstrated that MDMA, coupled with psychotherapy has remarkable efficacy in treating the symptoms of PTSD, a common psychiatric disorder in many hundreds of thousands of U.S. war veterans. Here again, if validated with planned larger Phase 3 clinical studies, this finding may represent a revolutionary new and much needed treatment for PTSD that sprang from a synthetic Schedule 1 chemical that was widely abused and also difficult to study because of Schedule I requirements. In this example, my laboratory was able to synthesize a sufficient amount of high-quality MDMA for clinical work prior to it actually being placed into Schedule 1. Had MDMA been scheduled more quickly, my laboratory would not have been able to produce it, and is unlikely that today we would have the possibility for this new treatment for PTSD. The investigator who we prepared the MDMA for had already requested bids for the synthesis of the substance from chemical synthesis companies, but they were far in excess of the cost his not-for-profit organization could afford. In fact, in the two other collaborative projects where I was able to produce Schedule 1 substances (i.e. DMT and psilocybin), again, no chemical synthesis firm was willing to produce a sufficient amount of material in a quantity and quality that could be used in human studies, at a cost the investigators could afford.

Some of the most difficult to treat diseases we face today involve dysfunction in the central nervous system. Unfortunately, most major pharmaceutical companies have abandoned research on novel drugs to treat conditions such as depression, bipolar disorder, obsessive-compulsive disorder, and others. These diseases have unknown causes, and the research is extremely expensive, with only a low probability of success. Yet the very kinds of substances that we are concerned with here today act in the brain, often by unknown mechanisms, and it is quite possible, as was the case with MDMA, that unexpected therapeutic efficacy might be found upon researching some of them. I am very concerned that new regulations do not, to use the old axiom, "throw out the baby with the bath water."

As another relevant example, when my son Charles Nichols was a new Assistant Professor of Pharmacology at the LSU medical center in New Orleans, he wished to carry out a study with a hallucinogen type molecule, but he had not yet obtained his Schedule 1 license. He asked me if there was such a molecule that was not controlled. There was only one, called DOI. It is the only molecule in this drug class that has not been scheduled, because it is the only tool that neuroscientists can still obtain without a Schedule 1 license to study the receptor target for hallucinogens. Using DOI he discovered, quite by accident, that it had unprecedented and potent anti-inflammatory properties, and his most recent research suggests that hallucinogens may be efficacious in treating cardiovascular disease as well as a variety of inflammatory conditions, including arthritis. His findings represent a potential major breakthrough for treating these conditions because current therapies either lack suitable efficacy, or else others, such as the biologics, are extremely expensive. Serendipitously, he had discovered a new potential pathway for reducing inflammation, including the possible prevention of asthma, only because that particular hallucinogen had not been placed into Schedule1. Had it already been scheduled, he likely never would have discovered these new therapeutic applications.

The cost of pharmaceutical research and development is already very high, and any additional regulatory burdens, such as working with controlled substances or their analogues, even as manufacturing intermediates, will be a strong disincentive to using them. The administrative and regulatory burden associated with conducting research using Schedule I drugs is a significant disincentive that would prevent pharmaceutical companies and researchers from exploring the value of these compounds. If a new drug molecule is discovered to have pharmacological properties that would likely lead to its being placed into Schedule 1, that finding usually signals the end of research on that drug.

It is difficult to convince agencies and investors to support research with unknown, novel substances; neither drug companies nor researchers want to deal with DEA/Schedule I requirements. It is simply easier for investigators to pursue studies that can be funded by institutions and government agencies. In addition, specialty chemical suppliers generally have little if any interest in producing any substance that is in Schedule I. Many of the recent clinical studies of MDMA, DMT, and psilocybin obtained their high-purity substances from synthesis in my laboratory under DEA-approved collaborative arrangements. Few, if any, laboratories and lab directors have the experience, proper licensing, and personal motivation to produce sufficient amounts of schedule 1 substances suitable for clinical studies at cost of production. Although the National Institute on Drug Abuse (NIDA) can provide small amounts of controlled substances to qualified and licensed investigators, their mission is to prevent drug abuse. Hence, they generally support studies designed to identify harmful effects of drugs, rather than research that is geared toward identifying beneficial properties of controlled substances.

When a substance is determined to be an analogue of a scheduled controlled drug, any research being conducted with that substance must stop until DEA licensing can be obtained to continue working with the newly controlled substance. Analogue designations have a direct impact on research.

I am particularly concerned that broad scheduling of compounds with no history of abuse or evidence of abuse potential, even in animal or in vitro models, will lead to control of compounds that also may be important intermediates for manufacture of medicinal agents. Regulations concerning use of controlled substances is an obstacle not only to their production as final compounds, but also their use in legitimate manufacturing processes. These controls are a disincentive to their use because they involve licensing fees, strict inventory control, and enhanced security procedures.

I believe that any legislative response to synthetic drugs must keep in the mind the challenges that scheduling presents for legitimate research, including possible research that might lead to discovery of novel therapeutic agents. I think these issues should involve discussions with representatives for numerous stakeholders, including academic and institutional scientists, as well as pharmaceutical manufacturers and enforcement agencies, so as to lead to a balanced approach to control that minimally impedes legitimate research.

Drug Control Should Be Grounded in Science

Federal drug scheduling law has given law enforcement and principally the DEA – not scientific experts or health officials – the authority to make final decisions about how a new substance should be scheduled. In the past the sudden appearance of a new psychoactive substance on the underground market has triggered the research and inquiry necessary to determine that the new substance represents a threat to human health, ultimately leading to its scheduling and control. It is my understanding that agencies within HHS, specifically FDA and NIDA are tasked with making recommendations to DEA regarding scheduling decisions. Their recommendations are based on a variety of factors, which include evidence that the purported compound was actually what was ingested, as demonstrated by chemical analysis and determination of plasma levels of the drug, as well as specific pharmacological tests showing potential for abuse, including for example, such tests as binding and functional activity at the relevant brain receptors, animal models of drug-self administration, drug discrimination tasks, and others. These agencies use the best science available to make a recommendation to DEA. These divisions also assess whether or not the new substance is actually causing harm to human health. These and other factors play into the recommendation FDA and NIDA makes to DEA regarding whether or not to place a new compound into schedule 1. Superficial comparisons of chemical structure resemblance or expected/predicted pharmacological effects are not a sufficient basis to place a compound into Schedule 1.

In the absence of these sorts of assessments, whether in human, animal, in vitro tests, or others, I believe it is unwise to propose scheduling novel molecules. No one can predict the potential of a new, untested molecule. It may have effects in humans similar to other structures, it may have completely novel effects, or it could be completely inactive. Sometimes changing a single atom on a molecule can dramatically alter its pharmacology. For example, adding one bromine atom to the potent hallucinogen LSD virtually abolishes its hallucinogenic activity. Prior to experimental studies showing that effect, no chemist could have predicted that dramatic change in biological action. Similarly, changing one methyl group on morphine to a three-carbon allyl group gives nalorphine, a drug that can actually block the effects of morphine. I also might note that bupropion (Wellbutrin) an effective antidepressant agent, can be considered to be a cathinone analogue, yet it has no abuse potential. My real point here is simply to emphasize that prediction of pharmacological properties based on superficial structural comparisons is not a reliable way to discern whether a new molecule will have abuse potential or will present a harm to human health.

As a perhaps more contemporary example, about 15 years ago it was discovered that ketamine, a dissociative anesthetic with significant abuse potential and addictive qualities, can produce rapid and virtually immediate antidepressant properties that last for up to about one week in some individuals. Yet, earlier this month, in the highly respected scientific journal Nature, it was reported that the antidepressant effect of ketamine is probably due to its metabolite 2-hydroxynorketamine, which does not produce hallucinogenic effects. Only experimental science could reveal that, yet the proposed new bills would likely have encompassed this metabolite as a proposed ketamine analogue, and would have led to its scheduling. Currently a ketamine analogue known as methoxetamine has been the subject of some abuse and has been scheduled in several states, yet with some anecdotal reports that it too may have novel antidepressant properties. New legislation that would broaden the definitions of analogues would likely lead to scheduling of a number of ketamine analogues, despite the possibility that legitimate clinical research might reveal novel antidepressant properties for one or more of them.

It is imperative therefore, that placing new substances into Schedule I must be based on solid scientific evidence; the possibility of preventing access to the molecule for research or potential therapeutic applications is too big a price to pay for a suspicion that a previously unknown molecule *might* have abuse potential.

Thus, it is important for any final scheduling decision to reflect a balance between law enforcement priorities and the scientific knowledge around these compounds. When scheduling decisions are being made, scientific and health experts both inside and outside of the government should have a formal role in deciding the appropriate schedule for an emerging substance, and if the substance has not formally emerged as a potential danger to human health, the suspicion that it might emerge does not seem sufficient to me to warrant scheduling.

Scheduling decisions should always be based upon science and available evidence. There should be a clear and compelling set of scientific criteria used to assess whether a particular substance should be controlled. There are literally many hundreds of thousands of synthetic compounds that could be made, many of which exist as "tweaked" versions of another similar compound. The scientific community as of yet knows very little about many of the most recently produced compounds, their pharmacology, abuse potential, or therapeutic potential. Under the federal Controlled Substances Act, there are no schedule categories for drugs that have no known medical value but also have not been proven to have high abuse potential, such as various hypothetical synthetic drugs. We should carefully assess compounds flagged by law enforcement, being sure to add only compounds with demonstrated psychoactive properties and a risk profile that clearly points to a public health and safety risk.

Compounds that have no demonstrated potential for abuse, let alone demonstrated psychoactive properties, should not be added to Schedule I. Doing so arbitrarily makes these compounds much more difficult to research. We must be careful not to sweep compounds into Schedule I that ultimately might be found to have therapeutic or scientific value, with all the ensuing red tape that can deter promising research.

Drug Control Should Not Exacerbate Mass Incarceration

Another reason for due diligence within the scientific/medical community is to ensure that compounds with no demonstrated abuse potential or real danger to public health are added to the drug schedule is to take into consideration the potential of needlessly prosecuting and incarcerating people for using or possessing these substances. Logic should tell us that the harms caused by enforcement of drug laws should not be more serious than the drugs themselves. Although individuals who knowingly manufacture and distribute substances that harm human health should be held accountable (ignoring the harms of alcohol and tobacco), I and many others do not believe that making criminals of users for simple possession is the appropriate approach. There appears to be a developing consensus that use of psychoactive substances should be approached as a public health issue, rather than a criminal one.

The current "war on drugs" has been largely unsuccessful in combatting drug use and has contributed to the United States having the largest prison population in the world, a large percentage of whom were incarcerated as a result of nonviolent drug offenses. Compounds that have demonstrated harm to human health, and those who manufacture and distribute them should be the focus of enforcement, not hypothetical compounds that some believe may cause harm, but without good scientific evidence.

Conclusion

In summary, I strongly agree that the proliferation of new psychoactive substances represents a great threat to the health of our youth, and regulation must be a component of the solution to this problem. I also believe, however, that drug control should be grounded in good science, and that experts in the areas of medicinal chemistry, neuropharmacology and toxicology should be involved in decisions about which compounds to schedule. There needs to be balance between the needs of research and enforcement, so that potential new therapies are not lost by restricting access to novel compounds. I do not believe that current proposals to expand the chemical landscape around already-known synthetic substances will be an adequate solution when completely new synthetics emerge that have not previously been encountered, such as the synthetic cannabimimetics. Finally, I do not believe it serves a useful purpose in society to impose harsh penalties on those who are found to be in possession of amounts of controlled substances for personal use; harms from law enforcement should not be greater than the harms resulting from use of these substances. Adolescents are known to be curious and to experiment, and most pass through that phase without serious consequences. Laws that impose draconian penalties and felony convictions on such persons destroy their future as productive American citizens. The focus needs to be on manufacturers and traffickers of dangerous substances.

_____

Mr. BUCK. Thank you, Dr. Nichols. We will now proceed under the 5 minute rule with questions for the witnesses. And I will recognize the Vice-Chairman, Mr. Gohmert from Texas.

Mr. GOHMERT. Thank you, Mr. Chair. I thank all the witness for being here. It is an important subject. And, Mr. Eckhardt, I know this is obviously very difficult for you. What a handsome young man you and your wife had, obviously brought a lot of joy. You mentioned that he bought it legally. You ever find out how he heard about this, and where he purchased it?

Mr. ECKHARDT. Connor was with a new friend that day. He had actually been offered—think it is on.

Mr. GOHMERT. Yeah. Think it is.

Mr. ECKHARDT. Can you hear me okay?

Mr. GOHMERT. Yeah.

Mr. ECKHARDT. He had actually been offered marijuana. He declined; he did not want that, he did not want to be around that. And as an alternative, the synthetic drugs were suggested and they were purchased at a local smoke shop, along with, you know, other tobacco products. And I think truly was viewed as a safe alternative.

Mr. GOHMERT. It was legal?

Mr. ECKHARDT. Legal.

Mr. GOHMERT. Yeah, so it must be okay.

Mr. ECKHARDT. And I think, you know, there is youth, find themselves often in situations of peer pressure, and he was declining one thing, and it was a way to concede.

Mr. GOHMERT. He was acting admirably. Relying on his government that if it was too harmful, it would be illegal, obviously. And obviously, as you and your wife have been doing, you have been raising awareness. If he had been aware of the dangers, obviously he was sharp enough, and moral enough that he would have turned it down, and just did not know the risk. Mr. Milione, how big is the market for illicit prescription drugs compared to heroin?

Mr. MILIONE. The market for prescription illicit or prescription opioids is massive. It would be hard to put a number on it. If you put it in overdose numbers, we are talking 18,000, 19,000 overdoses in 1 year of prescription opioids. With heroin, you have almost 9,000. That is a trend, heroin is trending up. You have a massive prescription opioid problem.

Mr. GOHMERT. So is the prescription opioid trending down, or just heroin trending up?

Mr. MILIONE. We do not see a downward trend in prescription opioid abuse or overdoses. That is trending up, not at quite the rate that heroin is trending up. They are both trending up; heroin is intersecting unfortunately, on that graph.

Mr. GOHMERT. Is it not interesting, as our Federal Government is forcing people to turn away from God, they are searching for answers in other places that are not so good for them? Do you know what the profit margin for a kilogram of a synthetic cannabinoid is?

Mr. MILIONE. It is a massive profit margin. So for maybe $1,500, $1,000, up to $2,000, you could buy a kilogram of synthetic substances that is a synthetic cannabinoid, and 13 kilograms of, let's say marshmallow leaf. And you can turn that into about $250,000, that initial $1,000 to $1,500 into $250,000 of profit.

Mr. GOHMERT. Dr. Nichols, you wrote an article in January of 2011, where you expressed remorse because someone had used your published research to produce a substance that caused six deaths. How could they have used your article to produce that? I mean, did you go into that kind of detail? It is hard to believe they could have taken your article and—what is that?

Mr. NICHOLS. The situation is, the chemists who were involved in making these substances are quite accomplished. I think many of them must have PhDs. So we publish in the open scientific literature, and I had been doing studies of ecstasy, its mechanism of action.

Mr. GOHMERT. Right.

Mr. NICHOLS. So one of the compounds we had made was called MTA. And in the assay that we used was a rad assay. It really identified compounds that caused the release of a brain transmitter called serotonin. And that does not represent the effects of ecstasy, but somebody, apparently in the Netherlands, saw that paper we published, and actually we had published that it was a potential anti-depressant, when we actually looked at it. They saw we had made it.

The synthetic methods are in all the published literature. So they simply made a batch of it, and ironically put it into tablets called flatliners. This was really the first case where—and I was really shocked, because all medicinal chemists who work in this field publish their work in the open literature, and if you work with cocaine analogs, or hallucinogens, or DMA analogues, it is all out there. The methods are on the papers. It just takes someone to mine that literature to find the kind of compound they want to work with.

Mr. GOHMERT. But you were not publishing the recipe or anything?

Mr. NICHOLS. It is in the scientific publication.

Mr. GOHMERT. But not in your article. That is what——

Mr. NICHOLS. No, not in the essay, no.

Mr. GOHMERT. But I am just saying. I think you blame yourself too much for that. But I appreciate the time. Thank you, I yield back.

Mr. BUCK. Chair recognizes the Ranking Member from Texas, Ms. Jackson Lee.

Ms. JACKSON LEE. Mr. Chairman, thank you very much. This is a very important hearing. I want to thank each of the witnesses; Mr. Milione and Mr. Smith, Mr. Eckhardt, and certainly Dr. Nichols. Thank you so very much. I hope I pronounced Mr. Milione almost correctly.

I was previously in a meeting, and I will have to go to another meeting dealing with criminal justice, but this is a very important hearing. Let me thank the Chairman as well, Mr. Buck. Let me also thank the Chairman of the Subcommittee, Mr. Sensenbrenner, and the Chairman of the full Committee, and Mr. Conyers, the Ranking Member of the full Committee.

I am grateful for the work that we have done to organize this hearing, and bring the use and abuse of synthetic drugs to the attention to the Subcommittee on Crime. We have several witnesses here today who will provide us with their own perspectives regarding the effects and dangers of synthetic drugs. My home State of Texas has been significantly affected by the proliferation of synthetic drugs.

Kush is a street name for the popular illegal substance in Houston right now. And it has caused great harm. It is a designer drug made from combinations of synthetic chemical, sprayed on plant material, then packaged like candy, smoked like marijuana. It has no constraints, no regulations, no guidelines. Kush is typically many times more potent than natural marijuana, and produces physical and psychological effects that are uncharacteristic of natural marijuana use. People who have used Kush have suffered paralysis, brain damage, heart attacks, and even death. Kush is but one name, or supposed brand name for the synthetic marijuana.

And law enforcement agencies, including those in Texas and across the Nation, have identified hundreds of names given to synthetic marijuana. This Committee hearing is important for that reason. We need to get the facts. Whatever we generate in legislation should be confined by the facts.

We do not want to expand the fishnet, if you will, on individuals who happen to be either attracted, addicted, or using this drug. And I hope that we will have enough facts in our record to be able to craft a sufficient Federal response to this very important issue. Mr. Chairman, I am going to ask unanimous consent that the rest of my statement be included in the record.

Mr. BUCK. Without objection.

[The prepared statement of Ms. Jackson Lee follows:]

Prepared Statement of the Honorable Sheila Jackson Lee, a Representative in Congress from the State of Texas, and Ranking Member, Subcommittee on Crime, Terrorism, Homeland Security, and Investigations

Thank you, Mr. Chairman, and Ranking Member Conyers.

I am grateful for the work you have done to organize this hearing and bring the use and abuse of synthetic drugs to the attention of the Subcommittee on Crime.

We have several witnesses here today, who will provide us with their own unique perspectives regarding the effects and dangers of synthetic drugs.

My home state of Texas has been significantly affected by the proliferation of synthetic drugs.

"Kush" is the street name for the most popular illegal substance in Houston right now.

It is a designer drug made from combinations of synthetic chemicals sprayed on plant material, then packaged like candy, and smoked like marijuana.

Kush is typically many times more potent than natural marijuana and produces physical and psychological effects that are uncharacteristic of natural marijuana use.

People who have used Kush have suffered paralysis, brain damage, heart attacks and even death.

Kush is but one name, or supposed brand name, for synthetic marijuana.

Law enforcement agencies across the Nation have identified hundreds of names given to synthetic marijuana.

Synthetic marijuana has become increasingly popular with teenagers as young as twelve and twenty-somethings.

According to the DEA, it is the second-most abused substance by twelfth-graders, and overdoses of the drug are increasing in Texas.

Synthetic marijuana has been linked to severe paranoia, psychotic episodes, violent delusions, kidney damage, suicidal thoughts, and self-mutilation.

Two weeks ago, a man commandeered a D.C. transit bus, then, struck and killed a man.

It was later determined that the individual who took over the bus smoked synthetic marijuana and PCP before the incident.

But, there are six other classes of synthetic drugs other than the class to which synthetic marijuana belongs.

A study conducted by the University of Michigan in 2014 revealed that synthetic drugs were the second most used substances amongst students in grades eight through twelve.

People are marketing synthetic drugs to our children with colorful packaging covered with cartoon characters.

Without knowing what they are ingesting, kids believe these substances pose no danger to them physically or legally because they can easily walk into a gas station or convenience store and purchase them with no hassle involved.

In reality, the dangers of using synthetic drugs are often greater than using the actual drug.

The physical and psychological effects produced by synthetic drugs are wholly unpredictable.

Those who overdose on these substances are also at greater risk of dying because doctors and first responders must first identify the source of the problem, preventing them from rendering the appropriate medical treatment in a timely manner, if, at all.

We all share common goals—to protect our children and shield them from dangers they may not be able to understand or appreciate.

We must consider all possible solutions, including treatment and prevention.

As we did when the House acted last week to pass legislation addressing the opioid epidemic, we must adopt comprehensive approaches to issues of synthetic drug abuse.

I hope the information we receive today will help us formulate appropriate and even-handed solutions that address more than just the criminal aspects of this problem.

Thank you.

———————

Ms. JACKSON LEE. And I am also going to ask that my questions for the witnesses be submitted for answers to comment. I ask unanimous consent, and my questions submitted to the witnesses that I may present.

Mr. BUCK. Without objection, so ordered.

Ms. JACKSON LEE. And I am going to propose a question to Dr. Nichols. I am concerned about making sure that we are not so broad that we in fact do not appropriately respond to synthetic drugs. And let me, by the way, in a moment of personal privilege, my daughter graduated with honors from the University of North Carolina, Chapel Hill, so you are elevated even higher in my eyesight.

Why is it important, Dr. Nichols, that the scientific experts in the fields that study synthetic compounds play a role in determining the appropriate response in terms of drug scheduling and other controlled measures? And might I ask that you describe any promising research that you are aware of on these issues.

Mr. NICHOLS. Well the legislation that I have seen in general basically tries to expand the landscape around known compounds, and I have done patent legislation, and I work with patents. And in patents, pharmaceutical companies will claim a genus of compounds. And in a recent case, there were 58 trillion compounds. So the possibility for harm is sort of unimaginable.

So I think we really need expert medicinal chemists and neuropharmacologists to look at these compounds that have been proposed for scheduling to really determine. I know I have seen some of the proposed bills, and they basically try to think of everything possible. One of the comments I made was, we are talking about hallucinogens, cathinone-analogues, fentanyl-analogues, and synthetic cannabinoid compounds. But what if a new type of drug hits the street? There is no legislation that would take care of a new chemo type.

So then, all of a sudden, we have another cathinone. Some Chinese chemist plays around a lab, finds something we have never seen before, and now we have another scourge. So the laws that are proposed really are sort of hindsight laws, based on, if all you have is a hammer, everything looks like a nail. I think we need some out of the box thinking in terms of ways to approach this that would cut off the possibility for new chemo types of drugs that we have not seen it, and would be more careful in circumscribing the things that we have.

Using expertise, there is lots of expertise in the American chemical society, in pharmacology societies, that could sit down and look at these and say, "These are problems, these need some evidence," rather than just casting a wide net that is going to create all kinds of problems. Many of the compounds may not even be harmful to human health.

So it is kind of an unfocused shotgun approach that I think could be much more focused on real problems with some expertise. And I just have not seen that brought to bear.

Ms. JACKSON LEE. Let me thank you. I know the other witnesses will have some instructive information that I will draw from your answers. Dr. Nichols, I think you have laid a landscape, or parameters, that we should seriously look at. We just had successful set of legislative initiatives on opioid, and I think it was based on a lot of thought, a lot of hearings, opioid and heroin. We passed a series of about 18 bills last week that all of us can find satisfaction in the way we approached it.

The Judiciary Committee bill did not have any mandatory minimums at all. It was treatment, and recognition of the vast problem. I want to make sure that we are accurately and appropriately addressing this problem, and I will take to heart, if you will, take under advisement, your very astute analysis dealing with the vastness of compounds and subsets that we should address to make sure that we narrowly address these poisonous synthetic drugs, and not have a wide reach.

With that, Mr. Chairman, thank you so very much. With that Mr. Chairman, I yield back, and I appreciate your time.

Mr. BUCK. Thank you, Ms. Jackson Lee. I now recognize the gentleman from Michigan, Mr. Bishop.

Mr. BISHOP. Thank you, Mr. Chair. And thank you to the witnesses for being here today. I want to particularly thank Mr. Eckhardt and Veronica for being here today, for your testimony. Like many of the folks in this room, I am a parent. I have a 16 year old son, and a 14 and a 10 year old. And this issue causes me great agony. And for you, my heart goes out to you and your wife. I pray for you and your family for what you have been through.

I thank you for your courage to be here. It is incredible what you are doing, and thank you for raising awareness. And I intend to take your message back to my district, and certainly to my family. But I wondered if you might be able to share with us what you believe, in your experience so far, is the most effective method of raising awareness, and what is the most efficient method in curtailing the use of synthetic drugs?

Ms. ECKHARDT. May I speak?

Mr. BISHOP. Yes, please.

Ms. ECKHARDT. Thank you so much for having us here. Obviously, it is very difficult for Devin and I. Not only did we travel overnight from California, but we are so passionate about this subject. And laws take time to change. They obviously need to change now. But getting that public service announcement, which is now happening with the opiate and heroin epidemic, getting public service announcements out there, recognizing that these products are available in candy form, in liquid form, in the vapes, in the e-cigarettes, in the marijuana type leaf, getting that message out there to parents. They simply do not know.

I said I wish I could carry—I have a book this big—that is full of stories, full of stories from people who have lost their children, either to death or to mental illness from using. People simply do not know. It needs to be taught in the classrooms. Teachers need to know. Physicians need to know. Nurses need to know. Counselors need to know. The public needs to know at large. And this is something that can be done immediately. Awareness, education, prevention.

And I would like to also mention that if you are 13, 14, 15, 17 years old, under 18 years old, and you become addicted to Spice, and it is very addictive, where do they go? There is not a place for an addicted child to get treatment, and this is a very serious issue needed to be discussed at another time. Thank you.

Mr. BISHOP. Thank you very much, Veronica, I appreciate your being here, and appreciate your testimony. Agent Milione and Officer Smith, I wondered if you might be able to address this issue. I, as a former prosecutor, have had an interaction with law enforcement over the years. K2 was an issue not too long ago. Hit the stores, it was in the local gas stations, at the party stores. I got a call from one of my local police chiefs, Chief Narsh from Lake Orion Police Department, who told me that he was trying to get it off the shelves but he could not do it because there was no legal authority to do that.

How do we get ahead of this? What do we do to give you the tools in law enforcement to prepare for the next generation? And clearly, these folks that are selling them in the stores are selling them with knowledge that they are being used in an illicit way. They are not just bath salts or incense. It is being used by our youth in a way that is intended for some sort of high. How do we get ahead of this, and what can we do as Congress to help and give you the tools you need?

Mr. MILIONE. Thank you very much for the question. As I mentioned before, we have already identified hundreds, not based on theory, but based on overdoses, deaths, law enforcement encounters, we are getting multiple every month. So now we are talking dozens every year. So, the most effective way to give immediate relief to our State and local partners and our Federal partners is get them into Schedule I. That would solve a couple of problems. It would give us the ability to get them out of those stores, to be able to stop it at the border.

But more importantly, we would be able to increase the cost of those that are trafficking it—not using it, trafficking in it—in the

United States, but then overseas, because they operate with impunity. That would be one fix.

Another possible solution would have to do with that labeling. In the same way that with anabolic steroids, there is a bill that you have to have appropriate labeling. If there is false labeling, there may be some kind of a false labeling penalty that would increase the civil penalty, and tamp down the incentive for these retail stores, convenience stores to have this in their places of business. So those are a couple of ideas, but we would be more than happy to work on any, providing any technical assistance in that area.

Mr. SMITH. Representative, as Veronica spoke to it, PSA and getting the word out on the street. And I believe Mr. Buck or Mr. Eckhardt spoke to the fact of these kids are buying this legally in stores. And again, thinking it is a legal substance, they are not doing any of the hardcore street drugs that we used to see them do: cocaine, heroin, marijuana. They are not taking this out of de facto ramifications that come from using something that they buy at their convenience store for $5.

Mr. BISHOP. Thank you both very much. I wish we had more time on this. I mean, anything I can personally do and I know others are the same way. Anyway I can help, I would love to be part of that solution. Thank you, Mr. Chairman. I yield back.

Mr. BUCK. Thank you, and the Chair recognizes Ms. Chu from California for 5 minutes.

Ms. CHU. Yes. Mr. Milione, the Controlled Substances Act provides for two mechanisms for controlling drugs and other substances. Congress can do it legislatively, or the DEA, in collaboration with the Department of Health and Human Services, can do it administratively. When the DEA takes an action to temporarily schedule a substance, retailers begin selling new versions of their products with new unregulated compounds in them. In your opinion, how effective is the current legislative framework?

Mr. MILIONE. Certainly we appreciate all the tools that Congress has given us. The challenge in this space is that it is a reactive process, and it is a lengthy process, resource-intensive process. And the same medicinal chemists, pharmacologists that do this analysis for DEA and work with our partners at HHS also travel the country. I think it is 65 different Federal prosecutions under the Analogue Act, as experts.

So it is a very reactive process. Scheduling temporarily takes, on average, three to 4 months, after harm has already occurred. Once we initiate that process, it is generally two to 3 years by the time HHS can do their analysis. So when you pile on top the dozens that we are getting every year, on top of the hundreds that we have already identified, it is like pushing that proverbial massive rock up a hill.

Ms. CHU. And what should Congress do to expedite the classification and scheduling of these synthetic drug analogues?

Mr. MILIONE. I would be willing to work with your staff to talk specifics, provide some technical advice, anything that would either streamline that process, or give us some breathing room and get the ones that we have already identified onto Schedule I.

Ms. CHU. Yes, I would love work with you on that.

Mr. MILIONE. Yes, absolutely.

Ms. CHU. Mr. Milione, in order to skirt Federal and State laws, many of these synthetic drugs are being labeled as not intended for human consumption, or legal in certain states. How are these claims affecting law enforcement's ability to prosecute synthetic drug-related crimes, and what could be done about this?

Mr. MILIONE. Well that is the evil brilliance of some of the traffickers. They are going to look at the law, the Analogue Act, and they are going to create something and put that on the substance so that creates a defense for them. So now you have a battle for the experts when you prosecute them under the Analogue Act.

So, one way that you could potentially fix that, that I mentioned a moment ago, is if you had some kind of a labeling requirement so that they are appropriately labeled. That would defeat that defense, but that is kind of in the realm of the technical assistance and advice or interaction that we could have to maybe talk about those in greater detail.

Ms. CHU. Mr. Milione, a majority of these synthetic drugs have been manufactured and imported from China. What has the DEA been doing to combat the manufacturing of these chemical compounds?

Mr. MILIONE. That is one of the biggest challenges, right? The manufacturers operate with impunity because the majority of these substances are not in Schedule I. Fortunately, we have a very strong and growing relationship with the Republic of China.

In October of 2015, they scheduled 116 of these new psychoactive substances, these synthetics, and as a result of our cooperation with them, they provided leads with us to identify domestically where gatekeepers and—not cartel heads, but cartel distributors— would be in the United States, so that we could work under our laws here in the United States to bring them to justice.

Ms. CHU. And how are these precursor chemicals being imported into the United States?

Mr. MILIONE. They are being labeled as research chemicals. They are being, like any other contraband, mislabeled and then sent in. And unfortunately, the majority of them, we do not have the authority to stop them. We cannot help our partners at the CBP, Customs and Border Patrol, because the majority of them are not scheduled.

Ms. CHU. And, Officer Smith, in the past several years, there has been an enormous increase in the variety and number of synthetic drugs available. The effects of the drugs can vary so greatly. As a first responder, what additional safety and health precautions do police officers have to take when approaching an individual suspected to be under the influence of synthetic drugs?

Mr. SMITH. Ma'am, from the law enforcement first responder stand point in general would be, law enforcement, fire, EMS, dealing with individuals on synthetic drugs, and I spoke to it earlier, it is similar to the effects of PCP on an individual. You know, they are very unpredictable to deal with. They can be very passive at one moment, and with the flick of a light switch per se, they are extremely agitated, they are very violent, and we are getting officers and firefighters and EMS responders hurt from the synthetic drugs.

Ms. CHU. Thank you. I yield back.

Mr. BUCK. Thank you. And the Chair recognizes Mr. Labrador from Idaho for 5 minutes.

Mr. LABRADOR. Thank you Mr. Chairman, and I will yield back 1 or 2 minutes to Mr. Bishop who has a few more questions.

Mr. BISHOP. Thank you, Congressman Labrador. We have got a thousand questions here and a very small amount of time, but I wondered if I might ask Mr. Milione—the DEA's Project Synergy found that millions of dollars in the sales of these synthetics were being funneled back to the Middle East, for what I assume to be terrorism purposes, or funding terrorism. Can you comment on that, and share more about that?

Mr. MILIONE. Sure. Project Synergy, it was a multi-year, multi-agency investigation, and you are right, about millions and millions, hundreds of millions in proceeds were going back to the Middle East; Yemen, Syria, Lebanon. We continue to explore that, we work with our partners at the FBI, and our Special Operations Division, which is a multi-agency coordination center.

But that operation resulted in the seizure of almost 7,000 kilograms of cathinones, cannabinoids, and a number of successful—hundreds of prosecutions. But we are still exploring that, and I would not be able to speak to some of the threads of those investigations on the money.

Mr. BISHOP. One follow-up, a quick follow-up—we know that this is not necessarily manufactured here, that in many cases, it comes from China, overseas somewhere. How is the trafficking handled when it gets to the Untired States? Who does it? Cartels or——

Mr. MILIONE. Well, on both the synthetic cannabinoid, cathinone side, but on the fentanyl analogues, which are the deadly, much more potent than heroin synthetic, there is several ways, but the primary way is, manufactured in China, sent into Mexico. Mexican cartels now are exploiting and capitalizing on the opioid epidemic in the country, obviously with their heroin trafficking, and they are taking the synthetic fentanyl, mixing it with heroin and other substances, and sending it across the border. Southwest border, couriers taking it into Lawrence, Massachusetts. Really, any part of the country is being touched.

But you can also get it directly from China. You can order it over the Internet. You can get this substance sent to you, delivered directly to your home. You can mix it with other compounds and then distribute it in the United States. It is a terrible treacherous world that they are creating.

Mr. BISHOP. Thank you very much for your testimony. I yield back to Congressmen Labrador.

Mr. LABRADOR. Thank you, Mr. Bishop. And thank you all for being here today. I applaud the Chairman for calling this hearing and taking steps to fight this epidemic.

Mr. Eckhardt, I want to express to you—I have five children, and I cannot even imagine what you are going through, and I want to express my deepest condolences to you, to your wife, and to your entire family for your tragic loss. I am sure it is difficult to be here and testify, but I greatly admire the courage that you have to testify here and to help us to more fully understand the true impact of these drugs, you know, on our society.

Mr. Milione, I want to follow up on some of the questions that were being asked. To your knowledge, is DEA working with Customs and Border Protection to interdict these shipments?

Mr. MILIONE. We are working with them as closely as we can and with the tools that we have, absolutely.

Mr. LABRADOR. Do you have cooperative agreements in place?

Mr. MILIONE. I do not know as far as the agreements, but I am sure there are MOU's that exist. But there is a healthy working relationship with CBP.

Mr. LABRADOR. Yeah. And you think that working relationship is functioning?

Mr. MILIONE. I believe so, in this context, yes.

Mr. LABRADOR. Can you estimate the number of prosecutions of synthetic drug manufacturers and distributors that have occurred in the United States?

Mr. MILIONE. I am sorry, I missed that.

Mr. LABRADOR. Can you estimate the number of prosecutions of synthetic drug manufacturers and distributors that have occurred in the United States?

Mr. MILIONE. It would be very hard for me to come up with a hard number. I would be happy to take that back and get that to you.

Mr. LABRADOR. Okay. Mr. Smith, how has your department had to shift its drug enforcement policies in order to combat the influx of synthetic drugs?

Mr. SMITH. The combating of the synthetic drugs is typical enforcement of any other law. The fact that we are running in a problem the same as Mr. Malone, and as Dr. Nichols testified to, is the ever-changing chemical make-up of these synthetic drugs for prosecution. Was made by the DEA and Dr. Nichols, just them tweaking one chemical atom of that synthetic drug changes the enforcement aspect on law enforcement's side, due to the fact of now, you have a chemical drug that was actually scheduled, now they change an atom, it is no longer that chemical, it is a new chemical, so therefore it cannot be prosecuted.

Mr. LABRADOR. Okay. Thank you. Mr. Eckhardt, is there anything that you have not been able to tell us, that we have not asked you, that you would like to say?

Mr. ECKHARDT. How much time do you have? Yeah, I think one of the things that occurs to me as this conversation goes on is, I would say at what price tag? At what price tag are changes being made, or being delayed? From a parent's perspective, from the general public's perspective, we would feel like, and the many, many hundreds of thousands of people that we have communicated with would feel like if something looks like a duck, it walks like a duck, it quacks like a duck, let's call it a duck.

We are down at the molecular atom structure, and because they change one molecule, it skirts our laws, and it is available. How many young people have to lose their lives to death or permanent disability? What is the impact on our community and our society as a result of that? And at what price tag are we preserving the ability to research these, or to talk about them or to study trends and statistics before we actually do something? Let's do something.

If it is not the right thing, we can always change it down the road as we learn more.

But I think parents and the general public out there need to be informed about this. We had no idea. We were not parents with our heads in the sand. We talked to our children about drugs and the perils of what they face as youth growing up in today's world. We did not have a clue about what is going on, and the more we learn, the more terrifying it gets to be a parent in today's world. We need help from our government.

Mr. LABRADOR. Thank you. I yield back.

Mr. BUCK. I thank the gentleman. The Chair recognizes the Chair of the full Committee, Mr. Goodlatte from Virginia.

Mr. GOODLATTE. Well thank you Mr. Chairman, and I apologize for not being able to be with you for the entire hearing. I did appreciate in particular your testimony, Mr. Eckhardt, and this brochure.

I have, in my experience here in the Congress, seen a few other people who basically dedicated their lives to trying to make their son or daughter's life meaningful, and I know that is exactly what you are trying to do in dealing with a horrific loss like you are. So, I very much commend you for that.

I do not know how much your foundation's research has given you about this, but—and it may have been asked already—but some of these products like K2 and Spice and Chronic that I see on the bottom of the brochure here—they look like, you know, regular commercial products, and that increases, I am sure, the opinion that people think that "Hey this must be legitimate. It is for sale here in this store."

What do you know about those companies? Are they legitimate companies that make other products, or are they just totally illegal operations that have this stuff mysteriously appear in various stores for people to buy?

Mr. ECKHARDT. Yeah, to the best of our understanding, there is no legitimate use for the chemicals, and the businesses that are proliferating these products out there in marketplace are not selling legitimate.

Mr. GOODLATTE. If you were to sue them, they would just disappear in thin air? They are not——

Mr. ECKHARDT. In the case with our son, we tried to discover who was the manufacturer, and were unable to get that, even though we had the packet itself. So there is a deep web, and it is not easy to go and identify. These are not products that are typically being made in some manufacturing plant with the name of the company out front.

Mr. GOODLATTE. Do you think they are made in the U.S. or made outside and shipped in?

Mr. ECKHARDT. Our understanding is both, both.

Mr. GOODLATTE. And how much cooperation did you get from law enforcement, from the DEA and others, in trying to do that research up that chain to find out who made it and where they made it?

Mr. ECKHARDT. From our perspective, the law enforcement and the people around us were very supportive.

Mr. GOODLATTE. But they were not able to help you go up the chain and find out who actually made that product that was in that bag?

Mr. ECKHARDT. Right.

Mr. GOODLATTE. Mr. Milione, you testified about how potent Fentanyl is even if it is just absorbed through the skin. What harm could this substance do if dispersed over a crowd of people?

Mr. MILIONE. It could kill them. I mean it would depress their—I am not a scientist, obviously, but we fortunately have much smarter people than myself on our staff that are scientists. And it will depress your respiration and it could cause death. So as was talked about, a very miniscule amount can cause death.

So one of the challenges obviously for the unsuspecting user is that they could be taking Fentanyl and not realize that it is Fentanyl and overdose. But then for my brothers and sisters in law enforcement, the first responders, and within the DEA, when we go in on warrants, it is a very, very difficult situation. Every time you encounter heroin now, you have to assume it is Fentanyl, because if you inhale it, it becomes airborne, you get it on your skin, you could have that kind of a reaction. So that is something that law enforcement all over the country is—and EMS, firefighters, everyone is concerned with that.

Mr. GOODLATTE. And that is added? Heroin is cut with that, and some other things are cut with that in order to increase the addictive nature of it? Is that——

Mr. MILIONE. Increase its potency, so it can be added——

Mr. GOODLATTE. That develops a reputation, people go back to it because "Hey, that was really"——

Mr. MILIONE. Well that is kind of the tragic part of it, right?

Mr. GOODLATTE. Yeah.

Mr. MILIONE. Word gets out that there is a very strong—and traffickers will do that. They will spike something very hot, so that when it goes out, unfortunately you will have overdose deaths. Word will travel, and that particular X product is very, very potent, so there will be a desire for that product. So it is mixed with heroin, it is mixed with other substances. It really can be mixed with anything, just to kind of expand its commercial viability.

Mr. GOODLATTE. Adding that to some other product, as dangerous as the other product might be, like heroin—adding that to it is almost tantamount to knowing you are going to be committing a certain number of murders as that is distributed amongst the populous.

Mr. MILIONE. That is——

Mr. GOODLATTE. Unavoidable that a significant quantity of this in the hands of the population is going to result in a certain number of deaths.

Mr. MILIONE. That is correct, and we have had success.

Mr. GOODLATTE. You have got to know that going in, right?

Mr. MILIONE. Yes, and we have had success with death investigations post-overdose.

Mr. GOODLATTE. How difficult is it to prosecute the manufacturers of these synthetic drugs?

Mr. MILIONE. When you were speaking earlier—here is the biggest challenge. The biggest challenge is it is reactive. Our success with any of the biggest cartels, the most violent insulated groups, has been with a proactive infiltration. To get them indicted, get them convicted, arrest them in the United States, or bring them—extradite them from another country.

The problem is in a reactive case, the harm has already occurred, so now you are trying to rebuild that. It is challenging, especially when the substances aren't necessarily Schedule I substances.

Mr. GOODLATTE. Thank you. My time has expired. Thank you, Mr. Chairman.

Mr. BUCK. This concludes today's hearing. Thanks to all of our distinguished witnesses for attending. Without objection, all Members will have 5 legislative days to submit additional written questions for the witnesses or additional materials for the record. The hearing is adjourned.

[Whereupon, at 11:21 a.m., the Subcommittee adjourned subject to the call of the Chair.]